How NOT To Be A Bully Target

A Program for Victims of Childhood Bullying (grades 3 – 6)

BY TERRY CENTRONE

To my good friends!
Terry Centrone

youth light inc.

© 2007 by YouthLight, Inc., Chapin, SC 29036

Cover Design and Layout by Diane Florence • Project Editing by Susan Bowman

ISBN   1-59850-012-0
EAN   978-1-59850-012-7

Library of Congress Number
2006934787

10 9 8 7 6 5 4 3 2 1
Printed in the United States

Table of Contents

Table of Contents

Table of Contents

(continued)

Introduction

This book speaks to children who are perpetual victims of bullies. Some girls and boys seem to attract the attention of different bullies again and again. They are repeatedly targeted by bullies who may use physical or verbal attacks to abuse them. Once these "targeted" children are rescued from one bully situation, another one usually seems to emerge. This is not to extend any blame whatsoever to the victims of bullying. Clearly, bullying can be devastating to a child. Bullying behaviors should not be tolerated in schools, and immediate interventions are often needed to stop bullies and to protect their victims. However, we should recognize that often the victims themselves can benefit when they learn to use self-empowering and confidence-building strategies.

The activities in the book are for girls as well as boys in Grades 3-6. The lessons will help children who are victims of bullying recover and become more empowered to guard against future bullying. There is a fifteen-part story that is broken down into separate units. Each episode is followed by activities that help build self-esteem and empower children with confidence. The story segments take the reader through Mya McGreggor's life experiences as she deals with low self-esteem and two girl bullies who have decided to target her. The main character's problems encourage children to become more self-approving, as do the activities. As readers complete the confidence-building tasks, they learn to accept themselves more unconditionally. Their new-found confidence can help them reduce the probability that they will ever be targeted by bullies again.

The motivation for writing this book came from many years of observing a disturbing change in the way students relate to each other. As a former teacher, I searched but found no other programs that specifically dealt with the damage bullying causes. None addressed the destruction of one's self-respect and the self-criticism that resulted. Most character education programs address bullying in a superficial way, if at all. This book looks closely at the cruelty of belittling others, judgmental behaviors, and negative self-talk.

Schools are unfriendly places to many children. The school day is often filled with negativity, criticism, and unsolicited opinions from peers and adults. Verbal abuse is so common in our schools that children learn to endure it on a daily basis. These critical words can cause damage. Sometimes people hardly know how they have negatively influenced a child with their words and at other times, unfortunately, the cruelty is planned. Within the school community, even teachers inadvertently say or do things that negatively affect a child's self-esteem. And the words of family and friends can also change a child's positive self-concept. Siblings often do the most damage to a child's self-image. All of these change a child from being confident to feeling inferior.

One of the most influential verbal abusers is network television. Children are quick learners. They hear their favorite cartoon characters or actors being judgmental and critical of their co-characters, for the sake of humor. The laughter causes them to imitate the sarcasm. They believe it is normal to talk back and ridicule others. Children are not able to discern that this type of humor is cruel, and normally would hurt the feelings of the weaker character.

By watching television, they innocently learn this talk. It then becomes a form of communicating with peers or family members. The results of this learned behavior are then heard in the home and at school, in peer-to-peer conversations. It shows up in classrooms, hallways, and cafeterias as disrespectful language and gestures. It is time to stop belittling others for the sake of self-empowerment.

School curriculums are not adequately addressing this horrific problem. In fact, tragedies in some of the best schools across our country have occurred simply because of words that were spoken by peers and adults. It is

becoming a national epidemic. Many unnecessary deaths have resulted from words that could have been avoided if children had been taught the unfortunate power negative words have. The time has come to stop this movement toward belittling others.

The sad thing is that over time, children begin to believe the misguided descriptions that have been directed toward them and they adopt these attitudes and beliefs as their own. This new image is seldom the one the child deserves. It first becomes a strong influence and then it develops into a belief. It crowds out other thoughts, especially if it comes from someone who is respected. This new description is often carried into adulthood and becomes a self-fulfilling prophecy.

How Not To Be A Bully Target can specifically change the way kids talk to each other. It can motivate children to improve their self-concepts in a pleasurable and interesting way. By using the activities in this book, students will practice positive self-regard and acceptance of their peers. Kind words and deeds will lead to success in the classroom and ultimately in life. Students will learn to see their own imperfections as unique traits to hold in high regard. As a result, students will transfer this positive self-acceptance to developing a kind regard for others.

There are many lessons in this book beyond learning to deal with bullies. Students will adopt a kind regard for animals, family, and friends. They'll look at parental and social relationships in a new and different light. They will see that friendships can develop between the young and the old. Students will learn that strangers often notice the good traits that are often overlooked by others they know. They will adopt the idea that we must accept others' differences and celebrate our own. Caring for others must continue for the rest of our lives. Standing up for

(continued)

oneself and being bold enough to refuse abuse may change future outcomes. They will look at the bully side of life to try to understand what motivates bullies. They will analyze the damage gossip can cause and will be encouraged to refuse to participate in its spread. Students will develop a new vocabulary in which negative emotions and thoughts are eliminated. Each learner will be encouraged to look forward to everyday with a positive state of mind. But most importantly, children using this book will learn how to talk to each other with kindness and respect. And as an added bonus, they will begin to treat themselves with kind words and thoughts. This is the real message behind the book. The activities that follow each chapter will help students learn tactics to diminish the use of belittling words. The book will involve students in correcting these issues in their own lives.

As a result of this positive self-regard, study skills will naturally begin to improve. Students will feel more confident in themselves and, thus, in the classroom. They will find a renewed joy in learning. They will become more independent as learners and feel secure enough to rely on their own problem-solving skills.

Students will begin to feel less fearful in all situations and will stop relying on the teacher or adults to intervene each time trouble arises. Throughout the book, students are encouraged to accept others for their differences, respect them for their talents, and develop a fond, personal regard for themselves.

This book will help students build a good self-concept and self-image. An improved self-concept will lead to a fond regard for others, to success in the classroom, and ultimately to success in life. Students will see their own imperfections in a positive way. They will celebrate their individuality and learn to appreciate and respect the uniqueness of others. Through reading, discussing, and completing the exercises, students will grow to approve of their own inadequacies and accept themselves with unconditional regard. Through positive self-talk in the classroom, students will begin to appreciate and enjoy conversing with their peers. They will notice how happy they can be in the absence of verbal abuse.

How To Use This Book

This text can be used throughout the year, or it can be condensed into shorter lengths of time. Teachers may pick and choose which activities are to be completed although some are connected and follow up on previous projects. It can be infused or be separate from character education curriculums.

Each of the fifteen units is introduced with a short summary of the story that describes an episode in Mya McGreggor's life. The summary is followed by a lesson plan. Teachers can use the lesson plan grids to see in succinct passages, the objectives, the materials needed, the outcomes, and the author's insights and messages. These short texts provide a window into each unit's focus.

In each new unit, a story episode follows the lesson plan. Teachers can read these passages to the students or copy and pass them to the class to read individually. Eventually students will need their own copies to answer the discussion questions that follow each story segment. These questions can be answered individually by students or discussed as a group. Students will also need the episode to help with some activities. Students can collect the story sections over the course of study and eventually have all fifteen segments to put together as a booklet.

The activities follow the discussion questions. Each unit has from one to five activities that teachers can choose from. Some are writing activities, some are visual projects, some involve chart making, and some are game-like. Each activity has a purpose that relates directly to the message in the story passage. Often the activities involve a class project that takes place over a period of time. The end goal of each is ultimately the building of self-confidence and self-acceptance. They all encourage students to feel good about themselves and their peers.

Dear Parents,

We are beginning an exciting unit of study in our classroom. It addresses bullying in schools, and is based on a book titled, **How Not To Be A Bully Target**. This book consists of a children's novel and a series of activities based on the novel's message. Its goal is to improve children's self-esteem and self-image. The project is intended to help students do better in school, be less judgmental of their peers, and enrich their own self-respect.

Every child suffers when peers or adults show them a lack of respect by name-calling, ridicule, or bullying. We all know how words can harm us, especially when people hardly know they have impacted us. The words of family, friends, classmates, and even teachers can unconsciously destroy someone's self-image, causing that person to feel inferior.

As time moves on, children often believe what people have said about them and they adopt these beliefs as their own. They may even carry these words into adulthood. No child deserves these judgmental descriptions. Unfortunately, they often take precedence over the child's own opinions, and the child begins to believe what others have said. This book hopes to change all that.

Having a positive self-image can lead to success in the classroom. It encourages an independent attitude toward learning, and ultimately leads to a successful, well-adjusted adulthood. The goal of this unit of study is to help children learn to appreciate their own uniqueness, and that of others.

It is our hope as we practice these activities in the classroom, that you at home will notice a positive change in your child. Perhaps it will show up as a newfound personal acceptance, or as pride in seeing a job well done at school and home. Ultimately, the program's goal is to set the stage for the beginnings of a confident adult.

Sincerely yours,

THE BULLIED LIFE BEGINS

STORY #1 SUMMARY

Two Girls on a Mean Streak

Readers meet main character, Mya McGreggor, a new 5th grade student. They learn of her first encounter with girl bullies, Bonnita Campbell and Franka Martin. Mya is bullied by the girls on the playground but chooses to defy them. This leads to the beginning of her long struggle with the two bullies.

Lesson	Objectives	Student Goals	Materials and Lesson	Insights	Author's Message
Story #1 **Two Girls on a Mean Streak**	Students meet main character, Mya McGreggor, a new 5th grade student and learn of her first encounter with girl bullies, Bonnita Campbell and Franka Martin.	Students become familiar with Mya's problem with bullies and empathize as she deals with her first encounter.	Students need a copy of the text. It can be read aloud to students, or they can read it silently. Small groups can also read together.	Mya is a worthy opponent for these female bullies who can be as cruel as boy bullies.	Bullies can be dealt with, but often there are repercussions.
Discussion Questions	Questions encourage students to look back for text support as they decide what motivated Mya to beat the bullies to bridge when she was warned to stay away. They think about why her classmates didn't stand by her. They begin to understand Mya's thinking.	Answering questions allows students to share heart felt thoughts and personal insights by discussing the text. They reason why Mya defied the bullies, look at her classmates' motivations, and see the relationship between anger and power.	Students need the discussion questions and a copy of the text to look for the answers. There is an opportunity for open dialogue among students in the form of large group conversations.	No answers are actually wrong, if students can support their thinking with facts from the story embellished by their own life experiences.	Good discussions can open dialogue between students and promote a change in thinking and behavior.
Activity 1: **Respect Tags**	Students read, fill in, and send *Respect Tags* filled with positive descriptive statements to their classmates.	Students become more selective when choosing words to describe others and themselves.	This is a pencil and paper activity. Time must be given to read, fill in, cut, and pass out the tags.	Positive descriptions empower students to feel good about their role in the classroom.	*Respect Tags* allow students to see how their peers view them in the classroom. Perhaps it is different from how they see themselves.
Activity 2: **Our Collection of Respect Tags**	Reading these phrases points out to students all the wonderful traits they have. Seeing them plotted out on a graph shows them that they are better individuals than they thought, and they become more accepting of themselves.	Students respect themselves more and realize that they are truly filled with goodness. They see that they are valuable, and that they can also treat themselves with kindness.	Students need the collection of tags given to them by their peers. They create a bar graph with their collection and write a character statement based on the results.	Acceptance and personal positive self-regard encourages us to become better than we actually think we are.	This activity is very empowering. It can reinforce goodness but it can also direct students (who may not yet be all that they can be) to believe that they can change for the better.
Activity 3: **Words That Act Like Corrosives**	Students understand that once they are exposed to corrosive and damaging words, the results often limit their accomplishments.	Students become more selective when choosing words to describe others and themselves. They see that corrosive thoughts impede accomplishments.	This is a pencil and paper activity that includes a copy of the worksheet. Time is needed to fill in the chart. The chart directs students to list corrosive thoughts and feelings. There is a group activity with a T-chart.	Hurtful words and phrases can lead to unhappy feelings, emotions, and thoughts.	It is time to stop damaging others and ourselves with negative self talk. Criticisms and judgments only stop us from succeeding.
Activity 4: **Bon Voyage Corrosive Thoughts**	Students celebrate the release of negative thoughts and beliefs.	Students realize the importance of celebrations as a way to commemorate special events, in this case releasing negativity.	Students need the T-chart created in *Words That Act Like Corrosives*. They also need celebratory items like confetti, balloons, and refreshments. Students destroy and dispose of the corrosive thoughts and celebrate the event with a Bon Voyage Party.	The destruction and disposal of negative thinking opens the door to a future filled with joy and self-acceptance.	We all deserve to accept ourselves with compassion and unconditional positive regard.
Activity 5: **Respect Tags for the Teacher**	Students learn to value the teacher as an educator and as a person. Teachers need to hear and believe positive statements about themselves, too.	Students have the opportunity to show how much they value their teacher. They express their appreciation using kind words and sentiments.	Students need a copy of the handout. They write positive phrases on the blank tags (about their teacher) and pass them to her.	If students are unaware and unappreciative of the work their teachers do to accomplish the tasks of educating, they may not value her.	Teachers often are so caught up in daily duties, that they forget how valuable they are as individuals and as educators of our future society.

Two Girls On A Mean Streak

The ground was quaking with a stampede of thundering feet as the recess bell rang. A group of fifth graders headed toward the playground. Behind Abraham Lincoln Elementary School in a small town in upstate New York, was a huge wooden structure filled with tree houses, bridges, and slides. The school children totally loved their playground.

It was just a few years ago that members of the community made it for the children to enjoy during recesses. Families got together and sanded, painted, and hammered boards with loving hands to give children an enjoyable, creative place to play. Normally the playground was wonderful, until today.

In that crowd of herding students were two best friends, Bonnita Campbell and Franka Martin. Their friendship was tight, and they refused to play with anyone else, ever. They headed for their favorite place on the playground along with their classmates.

Franka Martin was a short girl with brown wavy hair. Her nose was always turned upward. She wore fashionable clothes and often bragged about her latest purchase. Her attitude implied that she was better than others. Her best friend, Bonnita Campbell, wore only designer clothes with matching hair bands in her long blond hair. She was very tall and slim and planned to be a model one day.

Together, they were trouble. They talked alike, they walked alike, and they often dressed alike. Their favorite place on the playground was called The Great Bridge. It was a suspended walkway that led to a steep spiral slide. To get up to the bridge, they had to climb a ladder made of rope.

The ladder emerged onto the bridge from a porthole.

When they boosted themselves up onto the bridge, their reward was seeing the whole schoolyard from the highest point of the structure. At the back of the bridge, a slide swirled down in a twisted spiral to a soft rubbery pit. The slide was so fast that it felt like there were butterflies in their stomachs as they slid down and were dumped at the bottom.

The two friends quickly crunched across the snow toward the bridge. It was a cold, bitter day. Bonnita was first up the ladder, ahead of Franka. As she eased herself up through the porthole and onto the bridge, she noticed the new girl, Mya McGreggor, standing alone just above her. Bonnita couldn't believe her eyes. She watched the new girl walk shakily across the moving bridge toward the slide. Her hands were eagerly reaching out for the railings to keep herself upright as she walked.

Mya's very dark hair peeked out from under her hood as she looked down the slide. Her old pink hand-me-down coat flapped in the wind. She was just about to jump down when she heard movement at the porthole behind her.

Bonnita poked Franka's arm and angrily pointed at Mya. Franka just scowled. Mya turned in time to see the dirty looks she was getting and, without speaking, turned her back on them and leaped down the slide. She felt the butterflies float up from her stomach to her throat.

She landed in the soft pit with a thump. Unfortunately, she knew these girls did not like that she was on the bridge, and she prepared herself for what was to come. An unhappy memory flashed through Mya's mind as she sat there waiting.

Back in the classroom the teacher, Mrs. Braxton, had lined the children up before recess. Bonnita Campbell rudely marched up to Mya as she stood in line. In a nasty way, she said, "Hey new girl, you'd better stay off The Great Bridge because nobody is ever allowed up there, except of course, my friend Franka and me. It is our bridge. No one but us, get it? So stay clear."

Before Mya could say that she didn't even know where the bridge was, Franka came over and snottily asked her, "Why are you acting so creepy on your first day in our classroom? All you do is sit at your desk and look down at your toes. Can't you talk?" The two girls walked away and shook their heads with disgust. They weren't really looking for any answers. Franka turned back toward Mya and loudly repeated, "STAY OFF OUR BRIDGE!" Then with a pushy attitude, the two girls laughed at their own power and walked to the front of the recess line. The kids automatically parted to let them in.

The class was dismissed for recess and ran toward the playground. They sounded like wild horses, and separated themselves into lines as they scurried for the playground. Soon small groups were outrunning other groups, and there was a mad dash for ladders and slides. Most of the class poured up the ladders to three tree houses that were connected by pipe-like tunnels. Franka and Bonnita, of course, scrambled right up the ladder toward their bridge, not knowing that someone had beaten them there.

No one knew that last year Mya had won a trophy for being the fastest runner in her fourth grade class in Florida. She sure surprised the two bullies. She was the last person to line up, back in the classroom, and there was a big space between her and the rest of the class. The fact that she had gotten to the bridge before the nasty twosome really made Franka and Bonnita mad. They thought she must have taken a shortcut. She couldn't possibly have outrun them! But she did.

As Mya sat in the pit, they walked over to her. Franka yelled, "Who do you think you are, going up on our bridge? We told you not to go there."

Bonnita added, "Don't think about ever going up there again."

They made it clear to Mya that they did not want her on their bridge, their slide, or their pit. Tears started rolling down her cheeks as she stared back at them with fear in her eyes.

They enjoyed this. They loved making her squirm, so they began taunting her with a mean little rhyme, "My-a's a Cry-ah, My-a's a Cry-ah, My-a's a Cry-ah,"

over and over again until the other kids picked up on it and joined in. The teachers were talking about dinner preparations over by the bleachers. They didn't even hear.

As more tears streamed down her face, Mya slowly got up. She felt a strange strength come over her as anger raged inside her. She never looked at them as she slowly but bravely walked over to the ladder. Step-by-unbelievable-step, she climbed back up to the porthole and sat herself on the bridge once again. This was a bold act for someone who had just been humiliated by her whole class. Somehow, even though her insides were like mush, Mya knew that the only way to stop bullies in their tracks was to act as confident as possible.

Franka and Bonnita both put their hands on their hips at the same time as they watched her. Their mouths fell open. "HOW RUDE!" they both yelled. They were too shocked to do or say anything horrible. The new girl was defying them.

As Mya sat on the bridge with her head hanging down, she watched her tears drop onto her old, pink coat. Her sleeves got soggy from wiping her tears. She didn't want anyone to see how hurt she was. The cutting words rang through her brain over and over, "My-a's a Cry-ah, My-a's a Cry-ah, My-a's a Cry-ah." She just sat there with her back to the jeering crowd. Then the whistle blew and her first recess was over.

Two Girls On A Mean Streak

Discussion Questions

 Mya had a bit of a bold streak in her. Knowing that she was warned not to go on The Great Bridge by Bonnita Campbell, she outran the two bullies and waited for them to notice her on their bridge. Why do you think she did that?

 What do you think was the reason the other kids on the playground joined in the taunting rhyme, "Mya's a Cry-ah?" Why didn't they sympathize with her and stop the bullies from being mean to her?

 Mya became very angry with Bonnita and Franka as they belittled her in front of all the children on the playground. Instead of running off humiliated to cry alone in a corner, she defied them again. Her anger made her feel powerful. What thoughts do you think were running around inside her head as she walked up the ladder again?

Respect Tags

If Mya's classmates performed this activity in the classroom, their attitude toward her might have been entirely different. They would probably have gotten to know her better so they could send her an appropriate tag.

In this activity, you will be sending tags to your classmates. In the boxes, there are a series of respectful comments. Pick the tags that describe your classmates best and fill them in like gift tags.

Then, cut the tags up and pass them out like Valentine cards on Valentine's Day. You may wish to make decorative "baskets" to set out on your desk for your collection.

R E S P E C T   T A G S

You are an intelligent person. *To:* *From:*	**You love to learn new things.** *To:* *From:*	**You are a good listener.** *To:* *From:*	**Kids enjoy being with you.** *To:* *From:*
You are fun to be with. *To:* *From:*	**You have wonderful ideas.** *To:* *From:*	**You are funny.** *To:* *From:*	**You are a nice person.** *To:* *From:*
Everyone in the class likes you. *To:* *From:*	**You are so dependable.** *To:* *From:*	**I am glad you are in my room.** *To:* *From:*	**You are not afra of hard work.** *To:* *From:*
You are very kind to others. *To:* *From:*	**Your work is always done well.** *To:* *From:*	**You have great study habits.** *To:* *From:*	**You believe in yourself.** *To:* *From:*
Your ideas are so clever. *To:* *From:*	**You take pride in your work.** *To:* *From:*	**You are a good reader.** *To:* *From:*	**You always see the best in others** *To:* *From:*

Respect Tags

You pay close attention in class. *To:* *From:*	I am glad I know you as a friend. *To:* *From:*	You are a good person. *To:* *From:*	You never say bad things about people. *To:* *From:*
You love to answer tough questions. *To:* *From:*	You treat people well. *To:* *From:*	You are great in math. *To:* *From:*	You would never bully anyone. *To:* *From:*
You are a good friend. *To:* *From:*	Kids enjoy being with you. *To:* *From:*	You have a happy laugh. *To:* *From:*	You always play fair. *To:* *From:*
Your papers are organized and neat. *To:* *From:*	You stand tall and proud. *To:* *From:*	You are a good role model. *To:* *From:*	You make others happy when you are around. *To:* *From:*
You always play fair. *To:* *From:*	Your voice is confident. *To:* *From:*	People like you just the way you are. *To:* *From:*	You laugh easily and enjoy yourself. *To:* *From:*
You are a valuable person. *To:* *From:*	You are unique. *To:* *From:*	You try to help others in need. *To:* *From:*	You are always positive. *To:* *From:*
People look up to you. *To:* *From:*	People respect you. *To:* *From:*	You always treat others with respect. *To:* *From:*	You are kind and considerate. *To:* *From:*

Your Collection Of Respect Tags

ACTIVITY 2, STORY #1: *TWO GIRLS ON A MEAN STREAK*

Now that you have looked through the tags in your basket, you have a good idea of how your classmates feel about you. Perhaps you are surprised that they think so highly of you in certain areas. Read each tag over and take notice of who sent it. Enjoy the feeling that people respect you for the good things you do. Group them in piles sorting them by message, putting together those that are alike.

Once done, here is your task:

1) Make a bar graph using your tags, to see what characteristics you strongly demonstrate to your classmates. Notice the sample graph below.

Jim's Graph

You have great study habits. To: Jim From: Larry				
You have great study habits. To: Jim From: Mary	**Everyone in the class likes you.** To: Jim From: Pete			
You have great study habits. To: Jim From: Matt	**Everyone in the class likes you.** To: Jim From: Penny			
You have great study habits. To: Jim From: Winnie	**Everyone in the class likes you.** To: Jim From: Mrs. Braxton	**You treat people well.** To: Jim From: Susan	**You are a good person.** To: Jim From: Monique	**You would never bully anyone.** To: Jim From: Jake
You have great study habits. To: Jim From: Rudy	**Everyone in the class likes you.** To: Jim From: Leslie	**You treat people well.** To: Jim From: Sara	**You are a good person.** To: Jim From: Maxim	**You would never bully anyone.** To: Jim From: Mantel
You have great study habits. To: Jim From: Max	**Everyone in the class likes you.** To: Jim From: Mark	**You treat people well.** To: Jim From: Shariff	**You are a good person.** To: Jim From: Antonio	**You would never bully anyone.** To: Jim From: Jason

(continued)

2) Glue yours on paper, stacking them from the bottom up, in columns.

When you are finished you will see which ones you demonstrate to your classmates every day. Be proud! Take note of them and live up to each message as best you can. Enjoy what people believe about you and take them to heart. Accept them and live up to their message. You may even wish to work on improving yourself by actively practicing the other traits found on the rest of the tags. By adding these to your list of personal habits, you will find that others will respect you more, and that you will begin to improve your own self-concept.

3) Read Jim's character statement in the box. Now, write your own on your graph to summarize the kind of person your classmates think you are. Take note that these are the things you portray to your friends.

4) Glue your character statement and graph to the inside cover of your most used notebook. Look at it and read it over each time you open it to remind yourself of what others think of you.

Jim's Character Statement (based on his graph)

I am well respected in my classroom. I study hard and get my work done on time. I am very likeable and have many friends in the class. I make it a point to treat others with respect and am a person who treats others fairly. It is not my way to bully others to make them feel bad about themselves.

Words That Act Like Corrosives

Mya McGreggor listened to meanness coming from her classmates on the first day in her new school. They hurt her so much she began to cry, and then she was ridiculed for crying. When she heard the hurtful words coming from others, it made her feel unworthy and angry at the same time. She began believing what they said about her, and that is why she cried. She didn't want it to be true.

Have you ever said mean words like these to yourself? "I am not very good at this. I can't do it. I am not smart enough." Have you heard someone tell you that you weren't good enough to be on a ball team or that your work was not as good as others? Words like these act like toxic chemicals on your brain. They convince your mind that you are unable to do a certain thing. Then they come true. They are like acid that eats away your attempt to even try to accomplish something because you are certain you will fail. After hearing words like this again and again, your mind begins to believe this is true. Then you begin to believe it and say it to yourself.

It is time to get rid of this kind of thinking. Let go of corrosive thinking right now. Stop the negative self-talk. Once these thoughts are out of your mind and on paper, you are free from these self-doubts.

In this activity you will have a few things to do:
First, brainstorm your own list of cutting words and phrases in the boxes below. One has already been done for you.

I wish I had more right answers in class.

2.) Then, as your teacher makes a T-chart on large paper, plan to include your negative thoughts along with those of the rest of your class. On the left side of the chart labeled *Corrosive Thoughts*, there will be a list corrosive phrases that stop students from doing the things they believe they are not capable of. Here is an example to get you started.

T-Chart

Corrosive Thoughts	Corrosive Beliefs
I can't do this work.	Self-doubting

3.) You will notice that the other side of the chart is labeled *Corrosive Beliefs*. When we think badly about ourselves, we believe these negative thoughts. Below you will find a list of words to assign to these thoughts, as the left side of your T-chart fills up. Perhaps when you realize how awful these corrosive thoughts make you feel, you will see how damaging they really are. Then you will let them go as soon as possible and not allow them to roll around your head.

Corrosive Beliefs:

Incapable	Unwise	Frustrated	Upset
Embarrassing	Undeserving	Worried	Silly
Self-doubting	Alone	Vacant	Ridiculous
Left out	Hopeless	Absurd	Unsuccessful
Childish	Imperfect	Powerless	Vengeful
Fearful	Blank	Guilty	Burdened
Unworthy	Abnormal	Bland	Gawky

Bon Voyage Corrosive Thoughts

Now it is time to rid yourselves of corrosive thinking once and for all. In this activity you will plan a *Bon Voyage Party* for those corrosive thoughts you charted with your teacher in the previous activity. Bon voyage is a French term used when people go on a long journey. It means farewell, go forth, depart, and take leave. Usually, people have a party to say good-bye when someone leaves on a journey.

This goodbye party will be for the corrosive thoughts and beliefs you listed on the T-chart. Plan your own special ceremony with confetti, balloons, signs, and refreshments. You'll need some happy music, perhaps some speeches to say how badly these words once made you feel, and you'll need that original list of thoughts and feelings found on the T-chart in Activity 3.

Decide how you'll dispose of them. At the celebration, perhaps the teacher or each student can say a few empowering words that show the wisdom of releasing these defeating thoughts from your minds. Say your last farewells then rip up the chart and announce, "We hope to never think you again." Then throw them in the dumpster to be buried or burned, but not recycled.

22

Respect Tags for the Teacher

ACTIVITY 5, STORY #1: TWO GIRLS ON A MEAN STREAK

Everyone deserves respect, even the teacher. Very often we take teachers for granted and rarely remind them of how much we appreciate them and the hard work they do. It is a huge task to prepare all the lessons they present each day. Just think how Mrs. Braxton, Mya's teacher, would have felt if the class reminded her of her good qualities. Perhaps she would have been more interested in what was going on with her students. She may even have noticed who was being bullied and who was bullying.

Using the previous respect tags as models, list four character traits that describe your teacher on the blank tags below. Try to write and spell very carefully as you put down your ideas, so your teacher can easily read and understand your message. Once they are filled in, deliver them.

The first one is an example to help you do your task.

My reading has improved because you showed me how to solve my own reading problems. Thank you!
To: Mr. Bikowski   From: Jake

To: From:

To: From:

To: From:

To: From:

To: From:

23

Unit 2:

A PRIME CANDIDATE FOR BEING BULLIED

The Cooking Lesson

This story describes Mya's unhappy relationship with Momma. We learn why she feels bad about herself. This sets her up for being a target for being bullied. As she arrives home to her new apartment, she finds a picture of herself. It makes her feel depressed. Then Momma criticizes her cooking, and as she goes to bed, she feels lonely, rejected, and sad. She begins a relationship with a cat that is sitting on her windowsill.

Lesson	Objectives	Student Goals	Materials and Lesson	Insights	Author's Message
Story #2 The Cooking Lesson	Momma's critical comments about Mya's cooking make her feel unappreciated and imperfect in her mother's eyes. She feels alone in her battle against bullies.	Students identify with Mya's despair when she receives no comfort from Momma. They understand that the mother-daughter relationship is based on criticism. They notice the beginnings of a friendship with Meowy, the cat.	Students need a copy of the text. It can be read aloud to students, or they can read it silently. Small groups can also read together.	Throughout her life, Mya has been compared to Momma. In Momma's eyes, there is no comparison. Because of this, Mya is unsure of herself. This attitude even affects her cooking.	Parents can thoughtlessly dismiss children without realizing their special abilities. Sometimes they forget that children are fine just the way they are, without comparison.
Discussion Questions	These questions encourage students to explain why Momma compares Mya to herself, why the girl hates her own photo image, and why she showed no anger toward her mother. Mya treated Momma with loving kindness, even though Momma was critical of her cooking.	Students attempt to reason why Momma doesn't like Mya's appearance. They identify with Mya's despair over being picked on and criticized by her own mother. They explore the gentle side of Mya's personality.	Students need a copy of the discussion questions, the text to find answers, and an opportunity for open dialogue among students in the form of large group discussions.	Despair is an emotion that is difficult to deal with. We often suppress or cover it with other emotions such as anger and fear. We must address the reasons that have caused it to surface.	Sometimes we feel nothing goes right for us, and unfortunately, this is also the time we attack ourselves for not being perfect. Looking for support from those close to us is one way to deal with our sadness. We all need someone who will come to our assistance.
Activity 1: Picture, Picture on the Wall	Students develop a more positive self-image by studying a personal photo, drawing themselves in an enlarged version, and gluing a set of positive adjectives around the drawing to describe each feature.	Students become more accepting of themselves, their bodies, and their inner beauty.	Students need a pencil, crayons or markers, a copy of the worksheet, a piece of 12x18 white construction paper, and time to do the activity. Students also need a photograph of themselves. They learn to value each feature by gluing positive adjectives to a self-portrait.	Sometimes we need to appreciate our looks just as they are, with no qualifications.	We don't always realize how important our body is until it is not functioning properly. Now is the time to realize and appreciate the value of each wonderful part of us.
Activity 2: Redefine Yourself	Students write a caption for the drawing made in the activity, called Picture, Picture on the Wall. This new description redefines the student's image in positive terms.	Students view their image with uncritical eyes. They write only good qualities in their caption, noting positive traits, as they redefine their own image.	Students need their illustration, a sheet of paper, and a pencil. Each student writes a caption redefining herself or himself using positive terms. Drawings and captions are hung on the wall as reminders of these new descriptions.	Often we hate having our picture taken or looking at our own image because we see only flaws. We must view our image with kindness. We are unique. There is no one else exactly like us.	We must work to improve our self-image. Beginning at an early age, in order to love our bodies as we grow older, we must see only the positives. The parts we don't like make us unique.
Activity 3: Your Bests	Students realize that every part of their body has an important function, and they learn to appreciate the work each part does for them. They understand that body image is part of what makes them the person they are.	Students practice accepting themselves, their bodies, their thoughts, their responses, and their public image.	Students need the worksheet, a pencil, and time to answer questions as to why each body part and trait is likeable.	Children are often unappreciative of their bodies. This activity draws attention to all of these issues so that a negative self-image doesn't haunt them, as they become adults.	No one is perfect and isn't supposed to be. However, accepting and appreciating the parts of us that make us different is a very important step in liking our bodies. We must accept ourselves without qualifications.
Activity 4: Cook	Students feel empowered by cooking for their classmates. They take pride in planning and catering a banquet.	Students learn to be more accepting of their own and each other's imperfections.	Students need a copy of the directions for this activity, an opportunity to cook at home (or at school), a copy of the recipe for the dish, and a log describing the cooking. They will have the opportunity to present the recipe and pitfalls of cooking at a class banquet.	Students let go of criticizing others. They realize how cooking mistakes can happen so easily. Encouragement works far better than criticism.	Momma criticized Mya's macaroni and cheese, saying it was gluey. She never offered to cook. She never offered to help Mya, but she ate. She probably was criticizing something else.

THE COOKING LESSON

Mya McGreggor's first day at Abe Lincoln Elementary School had brought her to tears. As she walked home that frosty Monday afternoon, she prayed that her next day would be different. It was a long walk past the fruit market, past the gas station, and down her street, Washington Boulevard.

Mya finally spotted her new apartment. She and Momma had the downstairs of a yellow building on the corner of Washington Boulevard and Grove Street. Momma had given her a key to let herself in after school, but Mya saw the car parked in the driveway. It meant Momma was home.

They had just moved in over the weekend, and she expected that the apartment would still be a mess. Together they had done as much putting away as possible but there was still more to unpack. She opened the squeaky front door and entered the living room. She was right, it was still loaded with towers of boxes filled with clothes and memories from her past.

In the corner there stood an old fashioned wood-stove to help heat the house on really cold nights. Momma said the winters here were very cold, not like Florida's winters. The landlord had stacked wood by the kitchen door. Mya expected this would be a long, cold winter.

She scanned over the few odd pieces of furniture scattered around the room. It was all old stuff. There was a lumpy, blue couch and a mismatched brown recliner with a ripped right arm. The walls in the room were a dingy, drab yellow, and she decided they were in need of a good makeover. Most of the furniture came with the rented rooms. Momma said they were lucky to get any furniture.

She knew she had to be quiet. Momma was nowhere in sight, so she was probably napping in her bedroom. On Saturday they had set up both their bedrooms, and Mya was glad they did. At least they each had a place to crash. They planned to put the rest of their things away in drawers and closets throughout the week.

The lumpy couch was hardly visible because of the boxes filled with knick-knacks and photographs. Most of the pictures were of Momma posing for the camera. She loved having her picture taken. Whenever there was a camera around, Momma knew just how to look good. And she always reminded Mya that she was not as photogenic as her Momma was.

Momma always said, "Mya, you never take a good picture. Why don't you pose like me, just like the models do? Here, let me show you." Then she would try to pose Mya like a model in a magazine. She would demonstrate a smile and ask Mya to copy it. All this only made Mya feel unacceptable as she was. Why couldn't Momma just like Mya, imperfections and all? Her thoughts drifted back to the messy room.

Mya tried to move one of the boxes to sit down. Several pictures toppled onto the floor with a loud, glassy crash but nothing broke. Mya scrambled to put all the stuff back in the box before Momma emerged to see what happened, but she never came out. Mya guessed she must have been very tired.

Mandy McGreggor was a pretty woman. She was tall and lanky, the very opposite of her daughter, Mya. She had long brown hair and usually wore a ponytail. She took jobs wherever she could find them. She'd probably been out all day looking. The only thing she really knew how to do was wait on tables. Her feet always hurt from standing so much, so she took naps every afternoon before dinner. Of course that meant Mya had to do the cooking.

Mya's hands grabbed the pictures one by one and replaced them in the box. She managed to find one of the very few pictures of herself. It was taken on her last visit to the amusement park near her old home in Florida. Mya was standing uneasily in front of a bumper car. There was no smile on her face. She should have been having fun.

Not only did she look unhappy, but her hair was a mess. It was frazzled and smashed from the helmet she'd used for the ride. She had on an old pair of cut offs that were too small, and her t-shirt had a big blue stain from cotton candy, right in front. No wonder the kids at her old school picked on her. She was so tired of not fitting in. She wished all her troubles would end.

She studied the picture, noticing her sad eyes. Momma snapped the picture to show her how unhappy she looked when she was supposed to be enjoying herself. That was the day she found out they had to move.

Then her eyes fell upon her sleeve. She was still wearing her coat. The tearstains on the pink sleeve made it look orange. Her mind took her back to the incident on the bridge. She gave a big sigh and tore the coat from her body and threw it on the floor with an angry motion. The coat was another reminder of how unhappy her life was. In the kitchen, she found a note Momma had left her. It was short.

> *Honey,*
> *Make dinner, tonight. I am tired, job hunting. Mac and Cheese is fine. The directions are on the box.*
> *Love you,*
> *Momma*

Macaroni and cheese was always on their menu. But Momma was never satisfied with Mya's cooking. She was never satisfied with Mya, period. The girl began cooking dinner and at the same time prepared herself for a cooking lecture when her mother woke up.

She finished cooking and went into Momma's bedroom and touched her mother softly on the shoulder to wake her. She whispered, "Dinner's ready, Momma. Come and eat." She walked back into the kitchen, secretly hoping Momma would be in a happy mood. She decided she wouldn't bother her with the playground story. Momma had enough to worry about.

The tired woman finally dragged herself into the kitchen and sat down at Mr. Blanko's table. Mr. Salvatore Blanko was their new landlord. All the furniture was his. They had to pay a deposit and just bring their clothes and personal items like pictures, sheets, and towels. The pots, pans, and kitchen things all came with the apartment.

Everything was chipped and mismatched, but it saved them a lot of money not having to buy all that. On Saturday, Mr. Blanko told them that any wood they burned would cost them ten cents a log. He would give them ten pieces at a time and add the cost to their rent.

Momma put some macaroni into her mouth. Her eyes started to squint. "What did you put in this, glue?" she asked. "It tastes so sticky. One day I'll have to show you how to cook. Mya, you are going to kill us someday, the way you cook," she complained, "and I will be the first to die!" But she ate it all, every bit of it. She even wiped all the cheese off the plate with her finger and licked it off.

If she hated it so much, why did she eat it, Mya wondered? Sometimes it was too hard to figure people out, especially Momma. She was never satisfied when it came to Mya.

After finishing her homework, Mya put herself to bed. She liked having a room all to herself. She spent a lot of her time alone. She would talk to herself inside her head. She created her own imaginary life pretending she had lots of friends and an ordinary family. All she ever wanted was a normal life like everybody else. She lived inside her head most of the time, because friends were too hard to come by.

Her eyes drifted toward the window where she unexpectedly saw a cat staring at her from the outside. It was sitting on her windowsill. The cat blinked its big green eyes, so Mya responded by blinking back. She began thinking that she and the blinking cat had something in common: loneliness. Mya wondered if someday she and the cat would become friends.

The Cooking Lesson

Discussion Questions

 Mya asked herself the question, why couldn't Momma like her just the way she was, imperfections and all? Momma seemed to be comparing Mya to herself. What do you think is the reason Momma did this?

 As Mya looked at her own picture, she criticized her hair, her clothes, her total look, and agreed with her thoughts that she was not very special. She wished her troubles would end. Why did she feel so badly about her image? What do you think she meant by wanting her troubles to end?

 Mya was very kind to her mother by gently waking her up from her nap, yet Momma still disliked her daughter's cooking and told her so. What kept Mya from reacting to Momma with angry words?

Picture, Picture On The Wall

ACTIVITY 1, STORY #2: *THE COOKING LESSON*

 Mya found a picture of herself in the boxes piled on the old lumpy couch. The picture reminded her of how sad her life was, how much Momma made her feel imperfect, and how she needed something good to happen.

When you look at a picture of yourself, do you notice your imperfect parts first? Do you think you always take a great picture, or do you notice that your eyes are too small, that you wish you didn't wear glasses, or that your hair has had better days?

Sometimes our own images embarrass us because of something someone has said about how we look. Very often we take others' opinions as the truth, and we accept their beliefs as our own. Later those negative words come back to us when we hear them in our heads, as we say them to ourselves. Often we repeat those mean words with our own voices, and they become our words as we talk to ourselves. They become part of how we describe ourselves to others. Speaking to ourselves in kinder terms can make us feel good. We can feel more like the wonderful person that we are rather than an imperfect embarrassment. It's time to practice.

Bring to school the most favorite picture you have of yourself. It is better if you use a recent one that shows a full body image rather than just a headshot, so you can appreciate your whole self. Perhaps your mom is worried about sending it off to school, so pick one that she doesn't mind giving you, and your teacher can make a copy for you. Then you can take the picture home again. If there is still a problem, the school probably has a digital camera your class can borrow. The important thing is that you have a picture to use.

Study your picture for several minutes, looking at every feature. Notice these things:
- Is your face round or oval?
- Are your eyes narrow or wide? Look at the color of your irises.
- Are the eyebrows dark or light? See if they are curved or straight.
- Notice the texture, shape, and length of your hair. What is its real color? Usually it is a mixture of hues.
- Is your smile toothy or do you close your lips when you grin?
- Is your chin short or long?
- Does your neck show or is it stuffed down in your shirt?
- Are your ears visible or covered? Where do they sit on the side of your head?
- Notice your arms and legs. Are they long and thin or short and chunky?
- Is your body lean or muscular?

Now that you have looked closely at yourself, it is time to get to work. Here is what to do. Draw and color a picture of yourself on a large piece of construction paper (12x18) filling the sheet with your image. Look back at the photo constantly, like an artist does, to make your drawing as much like the real image as possible. Be sure to outline every feature on your drawing with black crayon or dark marker so the image is clear and not faded out.

Once you finish, cut out the descriptive words located in the boxes below and glue them around your image (like a diagram) to describe yourself. Connect the words and the body part with lines so anyone who sees this sketch will know exactly what you are saying about your features.

Friendly	Proud	Sharp
Bright	Bold	Striking
Creative	Intelligent	Athletic
Strong	Flawless	Energized
Gentle	Pure	Charming
Kind	Courageous	Attractive
Clever	Lovely	Wise
Graceful	Powerful	Muscular
Warm	Sturdy	Brilliant

Display these images in your classroom for all to see.

Redefine Yourself

Mya really needs this activity because her self-image is very negative. Between the two bullies' negative opinions and Momma's unflattering descriptions, Mya is quite down on herself.

We sometimes do the same thing to ourselves. We define or describe ourselves with words we have heard other people say about us. This is not right.

In this activity you will use the descriptive words you glued on your diagram in Activity 1, to redefine yourself. Your job will be to write a nice long caption to place at the bottom of your picture that tells everyone what a fabulous person you are because your features show this to all the world. Each feature, each part of your body, says to the world, "This is me and I am a great human being. You should get to know me."

Here's what to do:

- Write your full name at the top of your description paper and then tell about your features in complete sentences and in your proudest handwriting. This is a new definition of the positive, self-accepting person you have become.

- Hang your description at the bottom of your self-portrait, like a caption.

- Eventually, take your picture and caption home and place it in your bedroom where you can make it a point to read it before you go to bed each night. Believe in yourself and tell yourself about your greatness everyday. It will make you a happy person and better yet, a happy adult.

List Your Bests

Mya seemed to only think about her imperfections. She saw how terrible she looked in the picture, she noticed her bad helmet hair, and focused on the terrible blue stain on her shirt. She reminded herself that her classmates picked on her and how Momma hated her cooking. All these things haunted her mind and stayed with her, so that there was no room for good thoughts.

There are some great things about you that you probably need to take notice of, so it is time to make a list of them and think about why you need to appreciate them. Be kind to yourself and think about your best traits. This is a good way to learn to like who you are.

Here is an example:
I like my handwriting because *it is easy to read and people always say it is neat.*

Finish each statement on the next page. Reread them all when you finish and be proud of the person you are.

List Your Bests

♥ I like my eyes because _____

♥ I like my nose because _____

♥ I like my ears because _____

♥ I like my teeth because _____

♥ I like my hair because _____

♥ I like my skin because _____

♥ I like my hands and fingers because _____

♥ I like my legs because _____

♥ I like my smile because _____

♥ I like my way of thinking because _____

♥ I like my personality because _____

♥ I like my voice because _____

♥ I like my mind because _____

♥ I like my arms because _____

♥ I like my sense of humor because _____

♥ I like my laugh because _____

♥ I like when I talk in class because _____

♥ I like who I am because _____

34

ACTIVITY 4, STORY #2: THE COOKING LESSON

Mya had some trouble with cooking. Momma constantly complained that she wasn't a good cook even when it came to making macaroni and cheese. Of course, Mya just followed the instructions on the box, but Momma said it was sticky like glue. Perhaps Momma felt guilty about making Mya cook and used the unflattering words to distract her. Maybe she couldn't bring herself to compliment her own daughter.

Have you ever cooked for someone? Do you have a special dish you know how to prepare? This activity will allow you to cook for your classmates. You and your peers will prepare for a banquet, catered by you and your friends. Pick a day for all students to bring in a dish to pass. Put out the food like a buffet but below each plate, leave a comment sheet. After your classmates taste your dish, they can rate your cooking with <u>positive statements</u>, commenting on the great things about it.

Perhaps this will encourage you to cook more in the future.

There is more to do:
Write out your recipe on fancy paper. Write a paragraph at the bottom about the first time you made it. Who helped you cook it? Mention the cooking mistakes you made. Describe the occasion you were cooking for. Give lots of detail so the readers can get a good picture in their minds about your cooking experience. Use humor to describe your cooking mistakes.

If this is your first time cooking, tell about it and how you felt as a first-time cook. Looking back at your mistakes and having a laugh about them is very powerful. It takes a strong person to see the humor in failures. Laughing at yourself is much better than being laughed at. Nobody is perfect, and trying to always be perfect or meet someone else's expectations is very tiring.

These class written recipes will make a great cookbook. The teacher can put the recipes together in booklet form, and you can keep it for yourself or give it as a gift to someone special.

Unit 3:

THE AMBUSH

STORY #3 SUMMARY

___

The Girls go at it Again

Lincoln Elementary School is dismissed early because of a snowstorm. As Mya walks home, the bullies, Franka and Bonnita, ambush her. They pelt her with snowballs but fortunately, a shopkeeper named Mrs. Chinkley, saves her as she literally runs into the produce market.

esson	Objectives	Student Goals	Materials and Lesson	Insights	Author's Message
y #3 *Girls at it ain*	Students see the cruelty brought on by Bonnita and Franka, as they plan and carry out their revenge against Mya for a second time. They attack her with snowballs on her way home from school.	Students identify with Mya's plight. She feels totally alone as she battles Bonnita and Franka.	Students need a copy of the text. It can be read aloud to students, or they can read it silently. Small groups can also read together.	Sometimes when things look bleak and nothing seems to go right, we must look to find the gift that is always there. It may simply be a lesson we need to learn.	Even though mean things were done to her, Mya shows signs of being a strong girl and a good person. It takes a stranger, Mrs. Chinkley, to show her kindness. This gets her back on the right path.
cussion estions	The questions encourage students to look for answers as they talk about the bullies' snow day promise, what revenge feels like, and the negative influence taunting words have on Mya's emotions.	Students identify with Mya's feelings and emotions as she is bullied and attacked on her way home.	Students need the discussion questions and a copy of the text to look for the answers. There is an opportunity for open dialogue among students in the form of large group conversations.	Life sometimes disappoints us, and we realize how strong we are as we persevere through bad experiences. We see how important a good friend can be.	Mya needed a friend who liked her just as she was. Mrs. Chinkley proved to Mya that she was likeable, even during one of the worst times of her life.
ivity 1: *ing Blues*	Students write a fictional story to see the situation from all sides, including the point of view of the offender.	Through writing, students see bullying from all points of view. It is important to understand what motivates a bully.	This is a pencil and paper activity. Students need a copy of the worksheet to write about a fictitious bullying incident. They will focus on the choices that were made by all involved.	Sometimes, people are forced into a situation they do not like, but they must realize that they have options. If they learn from their mistakes they will make better choices in the future.	Our behavior touches other people. Sometimes, it is in positive ways and sometimes in negative ways. Our ultimate goal is to treat others, as we would like to be treated.
ivity 2: *s Away Blues*	This activity allows students to evaluate behaviors written about in the previous activity called *Crying the Blues*, students will transform unfortunate incidents into positive ones.	Through *Transformations*, students see that we must evaluate our motivations and select only the most positive behaviors.	Students need the worksheet, which includes space to transform negative situations into affirming reactions, a pencil, and the list of negative incidents from the previous activity.	Transforming negative situations into positive ones motivates good behaviors. It allows students to be the best they can be.	This activity allows students to be forgiving and compassionate with themselves. It gives them a chance to see the positive side of a situation that, at the time, might not have been so pleasant.
ivity 3: *ve lass ring*	Students discuss the incidents in their stories and the *Transformations* that resulted. This class sharing will change future behaviors.	Students realize that incidents need not have happened the way they did. In the future, better behavior choices can be made.	Students need a copy of their stories and *Transformations* from the previous activity. The group joins together in a circle to tell stories and share. Then, class discussions follow.	Students become more accepting of themselves and, as a direct result, more accepting of their classmates.	Hearing that people make bad choices one time or another helps us realize how imperfect we are, and that it's fine not to be so perfect. We must remember to make better choices next time.
ivity 4: *dness lage*	Students see, in a visual format, words that describe them as compassionate, kind, and interesting individuals. They create a *kindness collage*.	This activity will give students the opportunity to see all the good that is inside them.	Students need a copy of the worksheet that shows an example of a collage. They will need magazines, hand stamps, stickers, construction paper, scissors, and glue. They are to cut out words that describe themselves in a positive way, and glue them to the collage paper in an artistic format.	Think of Mya's apple crate as a metaphor for life. Each apple is like a new experience. They all have different tastes, like the incidents that occur in our lives. Some taste sour, some are dry and mealy, but most are sweet and juicy. No matter which we taste, our goal must be to get to the core. We must learn the lesson each experience teaches us. We must remember the good experiences and forget the bad.	It is empowering to see what wonderful gifts we have within us. We have the power to make lemonade out of lemons. We must appreciate our own talents and abilities.

uthLight, Inc.

THE GIRLS GO AT IT AGAIN

Mya stared at the snowflakes falling outside the classroom window. It was early December. She had been in her new school about a month now. She decided those snowflakes were the largest she'd ever seen. Of course she hadn't seen much snow in Florida. The snow was piling up fast on the parking lot below her classroom.

Most of the kids around her decided this was going to be an early dismissal day at Lincoln Elementary. The snow had started at seven-thirty that morning. During Principal Alexandra Dewey's announcements, it began coming down hard. It seemed every kid in school was checking the window to see how much snow had accumulated. The sidewalk and the parking lot were pure white.

Franka Martin and Bonnita Campbell, like everyone else, hoped for a snow day, too. Their eyes were glued to the windows and, at one point, they crossed all their fingers and closed their eyes and made a wish. They whispered something and made a secret promise. They hoped Principal Dewey would announce that school was going to be dismissed early that day. In their minds, there was no better feeling in life than getting a half-day off from school. Of course, an unexpected whole day was also very special.

All wishes came true about eleven-ten, just before lunches were to begin. Principal Dewey announced that the children were being sent home, just as soon as parents were notified of early dismissal on the local radio station. The road crews warned that the snow was accumulating too quickly and that it was getting dangerous for the bus drivers to get everyone home safely.

Franka and Bonnita looked at each other with the biggest grins. They both hammered their hands together for high fives and shouted, "Yes!" at the exact same time. By then all the kids were in a frenzy. They were darting around the room, congratulating each other, and gathering up their backpacks and coats.

Mrs. Braxton called the class to order and got the kids ready for dismissal. She took attendance using her emergency cards. These pink cards were filled out so students knew where to go, in case parents weren't home at this time of day. Mrs. Braxton was so frazzled that, as she put on her coat to take the kids out to the bus line, she had forgotten Mya had not yet turned in her pink card. Mya was too new to the routine and had never experienced a snow emergency.

In fact, Mya didn't know much about early dismissals at all and, particularly, that students might need a special place to go if parents worked. Of course, in Florida, there was never a snow dismissal, so Mya was in a complete fog about this procedure. And she only knew of one place she could go, and that was to her apartment where no one was home. Momma had said that she would be gone all day. Mya would be all alone that afternoon.

Mya had been at her locker in the hall gathering her coat and book bag and missed the go home-check. Mrs. Braxton got the students all lined up and hustled them onto their buses and sent the walkers off to their own destinations.

Mya trailed at the end of the line. She was beginning to worry. She knew

Momma wouldn't be home for hours. She had gotten a job at the Wispy Willow Restaurant, and would be working the breakfast and lunch shift. She was expected home by four o'clock. That was when Mya usually made it home, too.

Unfortunately, when Mya reached into the zippered pocket of her book bag, there was only an empty pouch. Then she realized she had not taken her key that morning, in her rush to get off to school. She had overslept and barely gulped down breakfast before running out the door. Momma had to leave by 5 a.m. to serve breakfast at the restaurant, so there was no one to remind her to take the key.

Mya never thought she'd be going home early that day. Her mind began to fill with fearful thoughts. Where would she go? If she went home, she might have to sit on the cold, snow-covered steps until Momma came home, and that would be a long, cold four and a half hours. There were no brothers or sisters and her father had disappeared from her life the day she was born. Her eyes got teary as worry gripped her.

She didn't really know any of the neighbors yet. They were strangers and, besides, Momma always said not to trust anyone she didn't know. She wasn't sure what she was going to do. She got more lost in her worries as she left the school grounds.

The walking was difficult. The blowing snow was so icy, it was pinching her skin just above her socks, and her mouth was hot and dry from being scared. She reached out to get a "snowball drink" from some fluffy, white snow, which had piled up on a nearby bush. As she picked up a clean ball of snow and brought it to her lips, she felt a painful whack, on the side of her face.

Her right cheek stung from the hit she took. It started to feel numb. She turned around to see who had ambushed her with an ice ball. The pain was piercing and the tears started pouring down her face. Behind a big snow covered bush, she saw two familiar heads under ski caps, snickering and ducking so they would not be seen. She knew who had hit her. It was the bully girls again, Bonnita and Franka. She tried to ignore them. She turned on her heel and kept walking, as if nothing had happened.

As she trudged down the slippery sidewalks of Main Street, she hoped that would be the end of the attack, but she knew better. She had made Franka and Bonnita really mad, on the playground, and she knew they were taking their revenge. They had found the perfect opportunity to get back at her.

BAM! BAM! BAM! BAM! This time a bunch of heavy snowballs hit her in the middle of her back with repeated thuds, one after another. They almost knocked her down as they took her breath away, but she stood her ground. Suddenly she heard two high-pitched whiney voices chanting, "My-a's a Cry-ah! My-a's a Cry-ah! My-a's a Cry-ah! My-a's a Cry-ah!"

She began to run. Her stomach churned inside as she put one foot in front of the other, faster and faster, trying to escape her ambushers.

The song kept repeating as it followed her down the street. Mya decided to "pour on some speed." She started to run so fast, she could hardly breathe. The icy cold air stung her throat and lungs, as her chest heaved up and down. The miserably cruel tune followed her. She heard their running footsteps behind her, and soon another snowball storm pelted her, knocking her down to the sidewalk.

By now her tears were gushing. Her mind zoomed out of control. Why did they hate her so much? What did she ever do to them? They didn't even know her. What was it that she had done to make them dislike her so much?

Then, a raging anger began welling up inside her, just like on the playground, when she climbed back up the ladder and sat on their bridge. She knew she had to stand up to them again, for her own self-respect. She couldn't let them know that they had gotten to her. Of course, she didn't care that her defiance was the reason they felt they had to take revenge.

She stood up and looked at them hiding behind the huge pillars in front of the Post Office and, without hesitation, stuck her *tongue* out at them. Then she turned and ran as fast as she could. She knew this would really get them mad. She darted out at top speed and left them way behind.

Mya's eyes were now flooded with tears. She could hardly see where she was going. She desperately ran for the corner, and that's when she abruptly cracked her head on something really hard. Mya fell to the snow-covered, icy sidewalk again, in a sobbing heap. She felt dizzy as she wiped off her face, looking for blood. She tried to see what she had run into.

Suddenly a huge avalanche of hard round objects began pelting her, but she knew this time it was not snowballs! It was apples! She had run into a stack of produce crates filled with apples just delivered to the corner market. Now the apples were bopping her, one after another. Could her life get any worse?

"Are you all right, Honey?" Mya looked up toward the voice. She couldn't see through her tears, and almost thought an angel from heaven was speaking to her. The voice spoke again, "You shouldn't be running like that, especially when it is so slippery." With that kind of warning, she knew she couldn't be in heaven. Mya wanted to see whose soft, kindly voice this was. It was a gentle voice, filled with lots of sympathy and caring. She felt herself being lifted up.

A woman began dusting the snow off Mya's back. The voice continued, "Come on inside for a minute. I have just the thing to soothe your bruises: hot chocolate! That's what my momma always gave me when things weren't going right." She turned to her helper.

"Jason, please pick up these apples and bring them in the store." She added with a smile as she looked at Mya again, "Jason is my delivery boy. He was in the process of unloading my apple shipment, when you came along and changed his plan."

She pointed at some stools over in the corner of the store and said, "Let's sit over there and get to know each other."

Finally someone with a kind word for her, thought Mya. She turned to look behind her as she was being escorted into Chinkley's Produce Market. She got a full view of the two angry faces of Franka Martin and Bonnita Campbell, staring at her through the store window.

As Mya looked at them, they began mouthing some words to her. First their lips formed, "My-a's a Cry-ah!" Then they both shoved their chins forward and whispered, "Big- ba-by. We-are-not-done-with-you-yet!" They smiled when they saw her face turn gray.

They shook hands and bumped hips and gave each other high fives. They had fulfilled their snow day promise, to get Mya back for what she had done to them on the playground. In their minds, she was taken care of, for now. They walked off laughing. This was their best snow day ever!

The Girls go at it Again

Discussion Questions

 Bonnita and Franka made a wish as they watched the snow falling outside the window. Then they whispered in each other's ears, making promises to one another. What do you imagine they promised each other?

 Mya guessed the bullies were getting their revenge, as they attacked her. She had been disrespected and insulted on the playground but she probably made them look weak, in front of their classmates. What is revenge? Does it truly satisfy a person to have revenge on those who anger them?

 Mya had been so brave, standing up against the bullies on the playground. Her courage, brought on by anger, caused the bullies to take revenge. Luckily, a gentle woman, Mrs. Chinkley, rescued her. If she felt safe at Chinkley's, why did seeing the bullies mouth mean words make her feel as if the words stabbed her straight through the heart?

Crying the Blues

ACTIVITY 1, STORY #3: *THE GIRLS GO AT IT AGAIN*

Unfortunately, Mya had pushed Franka and Bonnita too far. When she challenged them on the bridge, they planned their revenge to hurt her very deeply. The pain came from the icy, stinging snowballs and the cutting words they used to belittle her. As she ran toward Chinkley's Produce Market, she felt alone, rejected, and blue. She cried for all the bad things that were happening to her. She felt sorry for herself.

Her beliefs about herself were challenged. She found herself questioning her own value as a person. She even thought it was her fault that they hated her. But, she also encouraged their response by standing up to them, with anger in her heart, and disobeying them.

Sometimes, when we feel hurt by what others do or say to us, anger begins to build up inside. In order to feel better, we get mad at those who have hurt us deeply. This lashing out is called revenge.

When someone says something to you that makes you doubt yourself, makes you think badly about yourself, or makes you want to take revenge, remember this fact; people often treat us badly to feel better about themselves. In some crazy way, they feel good when they make someone else feel bad. In reality, they don't like themselves much. And they love leaving their victim feeling helpless.

In this activity, your job will be to write a fictional (not true, but possible) story. Use a bully attack as your theme.

See example on next page

Tommy Attacks

Larry Crosby was a good student. One afternoon, as the class readied for lunch, his best friend Willy called him to join the line. Willy was first and wanted Larry to be in front of him as line-leader. They always tried to stay together, so they could sit beside each other at the lunch table. Larry thought nothing of it and barged in line in front of Willy.

Tommy Wallman, who was just behind Willy, yelled, "Hey, you are a line breaker!" Then he knocked Larry down to the floor and held him there so he couldn't get back in line. He was mad because Larry had barged into the line and took the spot of line-leader. He wanted revenge.

Of course, the teacher, Mr. Elliot, came running over. He grabbed Larry and sent him to the back of the line for the trouble he caused. He ordered Larry to sit by himself at lunch that day and he took away his recess. Tommy explained how he was being a "good cop" and just doing his job, policing the line for line breakers. Mr. Elliot reminded him that policing was the teacher's job. But then he let Tommy get back in line where he had been before. Tommy received no punishment, nor did Willy.

Later, when Tommy saw Larry in the cafeteria, he went up to him and laughed right in his face. Tommy was very happy that Larry had to eat alone. He enjoyed "rubbing it in" so he did some bragging. He said, "You'll never guess who had lunch with me today so, I'll tell you. I had lunch with Willy. Bet you're jealous!" He took pride in knowing that he had caused all the problems and the teacher punished Larry.

Larry knew that Tommy actually wanted to get him in trouble because he wanted Willy for his friend, and was jealous about that. Tommy got his revenge and loved every minute of it.

Crying the Blues

ACTIVITY 1, STORY #3: *THE GIRLS GO AT IT AGAIN*   (continued)

Here's what to do:

■ First, plan out your story on this organizer by filling in the information below the headings.

im's	Bully's Full Name	What Happened and Who Was Involved	How Did the Situation Worsen?	What Lesson Was Learned?

■ Next, write your story on paper, and be sure to include all the details. Here are some reminders to help you write. Check them off as you complete them.

✔ Introduce your characters (with full names) at the beginning of your piece. Tell a little bit about them

✔ Reread as you add to your story, to make it sound connected.

✔ Change paragraphs whenever you change speakers. Put the words actually spoken, in quotation marks.

✔ Use nametags with your quotations to show who is talking. Example: *Mary said*, "What's for dinner?"

✔ Use transitional words to show a passing of time. Use first, second, next, then, soon, later, and suddenly to show time moving on.

✔ Describe the event and how it got worse in great detail. Tell it like a mind movie.

✔ Use your proudest handwriting and best spelling.

✔ Read it to someone when you finish. Make sure your message is clear. Continue reading your story a few times. Try to remember it for sharing in a later activity.

If Mya had known about this activity, she could have changed the behavior of the bullies. Ignoring them, or focusing on making new friends while on the playground, would have changed her fate. The incident at the bridge would never have happened. She wouldn't have cried the blues all over her coat sleeve. And, most of all, she would see that her own anger gave her more trouble by causing the attacks to continue on early dismissal day. If she looked at the playground incident from the bullies' point of view, perhaps she would see why they thought she was rude. Was she partially at fault?

In this activity, you will change the negative incidents that happened in the story you wrote, into positive actions or *Transformations*. *Transformations* help us to act in a more courteous way toward others, avoid conflict, and improve our self-respect.

In the story about Willy and Tommy, here's what we learned. We learned that if the boys had moved to the back of the line to begin with, no one's feelings would have been hurt. Tommy and Larry wouldn't have fought, Tommy wouldn't have laughed in Larry's face at the lunchroom, and the whole thing about who's to blame would not have happened. Here are some examples:

Negative Incident #1:
It is acceptable to break into a line to be with friends.

Transformation:
When getting in line, choose to follow the rules and never make people mad about where you stand. Being a line breaker is disrespectful to those already in line.

Negative Incident #2:
It is ok to laugh in a person's face, especially when that person feels sad already.

Transformation:
Be a thoughtful person who never makes others feel bad for what has happened to them. Be compassionate for those who are suffering.

Toss Away the Blues

Your task is to fill in the chart below. For every negative situation in your story, transform it. These statements will remind you that you can change a bad thing into a good thing, just by the choices you make. Write three in the boxes below.

Negative Incident #1:

Transformation:

Negative Incident #2:

Transformation:

Negative Incident #3:

Transformation:

Have a class discussion about these *Transformations*. Put your chairs into a large circle and take turns reading your stories to the class. Once a story has been read, each student should read aloud the most outstanding *Negative Incident*, followed by its *Transformation*. This activity will be a powerful change agent. It will encourage you and your classmates to make better choices about your behaviors.

As you listen, many of the incidents regarding the bully attacks in these stories will probably sound familiar. Hearing the hurt feelings and critical statements will seem like real life happenings. Perhaps this activity will stop someone from behaving in a mean-spirited way in the future.

Kindness Collage

You are going to make a Kindness Collage to describe yourself. You will only use kind words in this collage. Mya had a lot of hurt feelings. She would have enjoyed this activity.

Here's how to make one:

Cut words from newspapers, magazines, write them (in fancy lettering), use hand stamps, or type them on the computer in different fonts, and print them. Find words that are meaningful to you. The words should represent you, your thoughts, and your feelings about yourself. Be positive. If there are words that describe what you wish to be, add them too.

Fill the paper full of kind words, and glue them down. The more you put in the collage, the better it will look.

You can put a picture of yourself in the collage, hidden somewhere so that people have to really look hard to find it. Hang it in the classroom near your seat. You will love looking at these words that describe you.

Look at the box below. It is an example of a word collage. Yours will be larger and much fuller. Use it to help you design your collage on 8.5x11 paper.

Kindness Collage Sample:

MYA BEFRIENDS MRS. CHINKLEY

STORY #4 SUMMARY

The Hot Chocolate Saved Her

Mya makes a new friend whose name is Mrs. Chinkley. She owns Chinkley's Produce Market and invites Mya in to help her recover from the head-on collision she had with the apple crate. Mrs. Chinkley rescues Mya from the bully attack and the two get to know each other over hot chocolate.

Lesson	Objectives	Student Goals	Materials and Lesson	Insights	Author's Message
Story #4 The Hot Chocolate Saved Her	Students read about Mrs. Chinkley's gentle spirit. Her kindness allows Mya to feel confidence in herself. She begins to enjoy the woman's company.	Students identify with Mya's joy as she realizes that she has made a new friend, Mrs. Chinkley. She discovers that sharing troubles relieves unhappiness.	Students need a copy of the text. It can be read aloud to students, or they can read it silently. Small groups can also read together.	Mya begins to confide in Mrs. Chinkley and discovers a newfound feeling of confidence.	Mya starts to feel good about herself as she recalls her past. She begins to realize that she had good reason to feel sad and unloved. A lot of it was not her fault.
Discussion Questions	Students explain why Mrs. Chinkley assumes Mya is being harassed by boy bullies, why Mya doesn't think Mrs. Chinkley would understand about girl bullies, and why Mya's emotions make her worry about everything.	Students reason why Mya continues to be attacked by girl bullies. They see that this fact makes her feel so awful about herself that she cries easily, thinking she is deserving of these attacks.	Students need the discussion questions and a copy of the text to look for the answers. There is an opportunity for open dialogue among students in the form of large group conversations.	Crying is a way of releasing pent up feelings that have been suppressed. Mya cries about these issues in her life and now has a friend who will listen and comfort her.	Girls, who bully, attack their target by belittling in a cruel and intimidating way. The bullied girl takes the attacks personally. She often feels deserving of them. She feels part of the cause.
Activity 1: Forgive Past Cruelties	Students break down one of Mya's bullied experiences into three parts, like a cartoon. They then write a paragraph to the bullies from Mya's point of view. Their goal is to release her from the bully-caused suffering with a statement of forgiveness.	Students look at issues of blame as if they are Mya. They begin the process of forgiving the past and moving on.	Students need a pencil, a copy of the worksheet, and time to fill in cartoon boxes. They write from Mya's point of view. They tell about feelings and write a forgiveness statement, to release the power the bullies still have over Mya.	Seeing an incident broken down into its various parts allows us to pick it apart and decide that it really wasn't that significant.	It is important to forgive and forget. Forgiveness frees us from being the victim in the incident, always under the control of the perpetrator. It does not, however, condone the event.
Activity 2: Forgive the Past	Students remember a time when they were the bullies or performed a bully-like act. Their task is to understand it, forgive themselves, release it, and make it right.	Students realize that we all do awful things to others, and we might have done something in the past that was bully-like in fashion. But the past is gone and if we look at the situation again, we realize it is time to forgive.	Students need the worksheet and a pencil. Once the cartoon is drawn and word bubbles are filled in, the student redraws the cartoon to show what should have happened.	Sometimes we need to forgive ourselves for past mistakes to free ourselves from our own prison.	We must improve our self-concept and be more gentle and kind to ourselves. We must let go of guilt and punishment. There is enough of that coming from other sources.
Activity 3: Negative/ Positive Flashcards	Students practice learning new vocabulary that lets go of negative words and replaces them with positives.	Students practice with flashcards. The cards list opposite emotions, negatives versus positives. These flashcards encourage students to see things in a more positive light.	Students need the worksheet, scissors, glue, and partners. Once the cards are cut, folded and pasted, students practice memorizing the positive vocabulary with their partners. They recognize the negative emotions but recall only the positive ones.	We all look at the negatives of any situation and describe what happened with negative vocabulary first. It is time to drop this negative outlook.	As students work with the vocabulary cards, they begin to use these new words automatically. They try to be more and more positive when describing situations.
Activity 4: Positives Only	Students feel empowered by playing this game. It encourages them to recall positive memories and discuss them with a friend.	Students become more aware of happy events in their lives. The more they talk over these positive memories, the more joyous they become. They release unfortunate events from their memories.	Students need a copy of the worksheet, scissors, and a partner. Students recall and write down happy memories prompted by a list of statements. Once cut out, students discuss positive memories with a partner.	Students expand their vocabulary with very positive words.	Students become less critical of events by looking at the positive experiences they have had in their lives.

THE HOT CHOCOLATE SAVED HER

"Mmmmmm!" Mya said to herself as she gulped down her first few tastes of warm, chocolaty milk. She began to forget the bully attack. In her mind now, the snowball pelting by Franka and Bonnita was just a small, sad memory that unfortunately had happened. It needed to be forgiven and forgotten. In her heart, she knew they were wrong to treat her so badly. But if she kept angry thoughts in her mind, she'd be just like them. She'd be powerless. She'd feel that they had control of her. That was not what she wanted.

The hot chocolate was delicious. It made her feel better immediately. As she continued to drink, Mya let each mouthful swoosh around her tongue. Then she started to chew it before she swallowed. It was what she liked to do with hot chocolate. She almost forgot how she'd gotten to the produce market in the first place. At this particular moment, life was good.

Mrs. Chinkley, owner of Chinkley's Produce Market and now Mya's hero, was heating up more milk to make a second cup. She turned toward Mya and asked, "What were you running from, Honey? You must have been really frightened of whoever was chasing you. Why, you didn't even see that huge stack of apple crates out front. Was it a dog?" Mrs. Chinkley was getting a bit too nosey, thought Mya.

Mya was afraid to speak about what she had just been through. She didn't think a stranger would understand. She just shrugged her shoulders and took another sip. As she licked her lips, Mrs. Chinkley poured her a warm-up.

Mrs. Chinkley continued, "What's your name, Sweetie?"

"My name is Mya McGreggor," she answered. "My mom and I just moved here from Florida."

"Mya, that's a pretty name. It's different!" said Mrs. Chinkley.

"It wasn't a dog that chased me," Mya finally answered, not forgetting the earlier question. She wasn't sure why she began to feel safe with this woman, but she knew somehow they would become good friends, and she sure needed one. Mrs. Chinkley thought her name was pretty. No one ever told her that!

Hardly hearing that a dog didn't chase the girl, Mrs. Chinkley said, "Well I guess you can't stand this cold weather then, coming from Florida. It must be a shock to your system wintering here in New York State. What does your momma do?"

"Oh, she just got a new job. She does just about everything but she is best at being a waitress. She works at the Wispy Willow Restaurant." Then without thinking, Mya began telling Mrs. Chinkley why she crashed herself into the apple crates. She figured she owed her that.

"I was on my way home from school. They let us out early because of the snow. I was chased by some kids." She said it very casually, as if it was natural to be chased. She went on, "I am not sure if my momma is home from work yet." Mya second guessed herself and thought she might have given out too much information.

Mrs. Chinkley definitely had been listening and picked up on what Mya had said. "You mean no one is at home and you have the afternoon off from school? You say some children were chasing you? Kids are so mean to each other these days! Oh it doesn't matter, Mya, you can stay here the rest of the afternoon. I have plenty of work around the store if you'd like stay here to pass the time." She went on, "I have been looking for someone to sweep up around the market." She pointed to a sign in the store window that read, "Help Wanted."

If you wish to call your mother to let her know where you are, you may use the phone over there," Mrs. Chinkley continued. "I know if you were my daughter, I would want to know where you were and that you were safe. Probably those boys are gone anyway. Boys always chase girls at your age."

Mya wasn't about to tell the woman that it wasn't boys chasing her but she didn't think Mrs. Chinkley would understand, so she didn't correct her. She noticed how warm and thoughtful this woman was. Not at all like her mother or her schoolmates. Mya sometimes felt that she was bringing herself up and her mother, too. She was sure Momma was not even worried about her in this snowstorm, but instead was probably thinking of herself as usual. Mya imagined her trying to make a good impression so she would get good tips from her customers.

Mya thought that she could be sick in bed and her mother would probably be more worried about her chipped nail polish. She never took Mya seriously. Momma thought of Mya as the strong one in the family. Usually, Momma worried about how she looked and what people thought of her, rather than what Mya felt or worried about. Momma always called Mya her "big grown-up girl."

Lately this was getting to Mya. It seemed she was constantly feeling worried and on the verge of crying. She had become the crybaby in the family, just like Franka and Bonnita had said. Unfortunately, they were right about that.

Mya sometimes felt she and Momma weren't even related. She guessed she had been born with all the crying genes in the family and Momma got none, except for one time.

One late night, Momma had gotten a call from Mya's daddy while they were in Florida. It was just before they moved to New York. It woke Mya up. She heard Momma answer the call in her bedroom. Mya listened at the door in case it was bad news and heard Momma say, "Jack?" She had a worried tone in her voice.

Mya didn't know her daddy at all, but she knew his name. Suddenly Momma's voice became very loud and some curse words came out of her mouth. Mya hadn't heard her say words like that in a long time, not since she lost her job at the Home Fry Diner when she spilled eggs on a customer. She said the man was being mean to her and said awful things.

Then after more swearing and yelling, the phone was thrown across the room and it hit the door and bounced to the floor. Mya could hear the hum of the phone as Momma began to sob. Then she heard a bottle clink and some liquid being poured into a glass. That's when Momma really started crying and she cried the rest of the night.

It was a very sad memory. Mya was afraid to go in and comfort Momma. She never wanted to be comforted. She would probably just push Mya away so Mya positioned herself on the floor outside the door, and listened until Momma fell asleep. The next morning, when Mya got up to go to the bathroom, Momma came out of her room and went to the kitchen to make coffee. She never even knew Mya had slept outside her door all night, like a watchdog. Momma never mentioned the phone call to Mya.

The next thing that happened was that they moved! Mya just figured that her daddy must be a really mean man to call Momma after a whole lot of years and make her cry most of the night. Whatever he said must have really scared Momma. That next day, she decided they would move far away. Mya thought it was to get away from him.

Mya's thoughts came back to the present time as she sat finishing her hot chocolate at Chinkley's. She realized that something special had happened to her that day. What started out as a bad day, being chased then pummeled with snowballs, and finally taunted with hurting words, had turned into the first wonderful day she'd had since she moved to town. She had just gotten two cups of the best hot chocolate she'd ever had. And without even asking or searching, she was offered an after-school job. What could be better?

And more importantly, Louise Chinkley, her new boss, had saved her from being attacked by the two bullies, Franka and Bonnita. But best of all, she had made a true friend, in what seemed to be an unfriendly town.

As Mya started sweeping the floor, she realized how much she loved sweeping. She found herself hoping that her luck was turning around and that maybe she wouldn't always be a crybaby.

Discussion Questions

 Why did Mrs. Chinkley automatically think that boys were chasing Mya and pelting her with snowballs?

 Why did Mya feel Mrs. Chinkley wouldn't understand if she mentioned that girls were doing the bullying?

 Momma saw Mya as the strong one in the family. She was Momma's big grown-up girl. Momma thought Mya was serious and always in control of every situation. But Mya decided that she wasn't strong at all. She was constantly feeling worried and on the verge of tears. She felt she was the crybaby of the family. These two beliefs are opposite each other. Can you explain how this could be?

Forgive Past Cruelties

Think back to the story when Bonnita and Franka did very cruel things to Mya. Remember the cutting words and actions that made her feel small, frightened, and beaten down? These memories will be part of your first activity.

Here is your task:
Draw cartoon-like pictures of the playground attack that Mya suffered through in story #1. Draw the incident as if it happened in three parts, the beginning, middle, and end. Use lots of detail in your drawing and add speech bubbles to write what was said. You can look back into the story to make sure your information is accurate.

Mya and the Bullies

Beginning	Middle	End

As Mya sat in the market drinking her hot chocolate, she slowly began to forget about the bully attack. This was a good thing to do. But Mya wasn't able to let go of the label they gave her, "Mya's a Cry-ah." She began to believe what they said about her, and saw herself as a crybaby.

Let's take a lesson from this and learn to stop blaming people for the cruelty they may have caused us in the past. When we keep going over and over the mean behaviors in our minds, we become the victim. The words people used to make us feel bad continue making us feel bad, even when the problem happened long ago and these people are nowhere around. We let the words pop in our heads, and they hurt us over and over as we remember them.

Forgive Past Cruelties

Here is the next task:

Look back at your cartoon. Imagine that you are speaking to the bullies from Mya's point of view. Pretend you are Mya.

> – Write a note to the bullies about what they did, in the box below.
>
> – First, tell them how they made you (Mya) feel.
>
> – Then, write a statement of forgiveness to release them.

Here is an example:

> Bonnita and Franka,
> When you attacked me with your snowballs, you hurt my body and my feelings. You belittled me and made me feel hated. However, I forgive you for what you did because I don't want to punish myself any longer by thinking about it. I don't want to keep remembering how bad I felt. You missed out on having a really good friend in me.

Forgiveness Statement

Mya's point of view:

Afterthought:

Just imagine Mya reading over your statement. When she finishes, she lets it go in the wind. It flies up like a helium balloon. It sails off into the clouds, becoming smaller and smaller until it disappears. She smiles. She thanks you for helping her get over the attack. She is done remembering past cruelties.

Think back to a time in your past when you did something that you are ashamed of. Perhaps with words you used, you hurt someone very badly. You may have acted mean or naughty and now when you think back on it, you feel ashamed or embarrassed. If you acted badly while in a group of kids at the expense of others, hurting someone's feelings with cutting words, you may wish to forgive yourself for doing that.

Here are your two tasks:
In the boxes below, draw a cartoon-like picture of that incident using great detail and, in speech bubbles, write what was said.

Beginning	Middle	End

Now it is time to stop blaming yourself for your unfortunate behavior. After all, you know that it was a poor choice and you can forgive yourself for not knowing better. You now know how words and actions can really hurt others.

Redraw the event and show how you wish it had happened. Then stop the blame, forgive it and forget it. Perhaps someday you will have an opportunity to undo what was done. Be ready to apologize to the person you once hurt.

Beginning	Middle	End

Negative/Positive Flashcards

Bonnita and Franka could make good use of these flashcards. If they had them and practiced with them, perhaps they would have been nicer to Mya and to themselves.

The cards on the next two pages show 25 positive and negative feelings or emotions. They are opposites. Your mission is to drop the negatives from your vocabulary, and use only the positive ones. If you adopt these positive words, you will definitely change your life for the better.

This is your task:

■ Read over the list below and cut the cards out as pairs, across the centerline.

■ Fold them on that line and paste them back-to-back to make a packet of cards that flip over, one side negative and the other positive.

■ Read them over and over until you have them memorized.

■ Find a partner to play with. Spread the cards on your desk, negative side up. Take turns choosing a word and recall only the positive word that is face down.

■ Flip it and see if you are right. If you are, total up the letters found in the positive word as your points. The winner is the one who has the most points when all cards are flipped. If you don't guess correctly, put the card back down with the negative side showing. To make it interesting you can subtract the negative letter points if you guess wrong.

It is now up to you to make the positive words part of your everyday vocabulary.

Negative Emotions	Positive Emotions
AFRAID	**CONFIDENT**
HATEFUL	**FORGIVING**
BELITTLED	**PRAISED**
BLAMED	**INNOCENT**
CHURNING INSIDE	**CALM**
CRUEL	**KIND**
REJECTED	**ACCEPTED**
RIDICULED	**APPROVED OF**
VIOLENT	**PEACEFUL**
BULLYING	**RESPECTFUL**
WORTHLESS	**VALUABLE**
PESTY	**SUPPORTIVE**

SAD	**JOYOUS**
UNWORTHY	**DESERVING**
NAUGHTY	**COOPERATIVE**
UNRULY	**WELL BEHAVED**
STUBBORN	**WILLING**
STUCK-UP	**FRIENDLY**
UNINTELLIGENT	**CLEVER**
EMBARRASSED	**CERTAIN**
GAWKY	**POISED**
CLUMSY	**GRACEFUL**
DULL	**BRILLIANT**
ILL-AT-EASE	**COMFORTABLE**
SELF-CONSCIOUS	**SELF-ACCEPTING**

Positives Only

ACTIVITY 4, STORY #4: *THE HOT CHOCOLATE SAVED HER*

This activity consists of writing a list of positive memories. There is no room for sad memories here. We often find it hard to recall happy memories. Bad memories are easy to recall. As you work with statements like these, you will begin to let go of the negative and focus on the positive.

Here is what to do with these statements:

■ Read each statement to yourself.

■ Think about an incident that fits each positive description. Recall all the good memories and write them down after each statement. Use true facts from your life. Then cut them out.

Example:

I felt happy when **my mother told me how much my writing reminded her of her favorite author.**

When you are finished with these statements:

■ Turn your list face down on your desk and then find a partner.

■ Your partner will have a list ready too. Make sure you are near each other.

■ Take turns reading a statement at a time, recalling the memory with your friend.

■ Continue until you have both finished talking about the good things that have happened in your life.

I felt accepted when _____

I was honored by _____

I was complemented for _____

I was recognized by a teacher for my _____

I felt included when _____

I feel cherished by _____

I feel appreciated when I _____

I feel happy about _____

I feel empowered when I _____

Forgiving makes me feel like _____

I am most peaceful when _____

I am liked by _____

I celebrate my good work by _____

I approve of my _____

I feel respectful toward _____

I admire *(who)* _____ because _____

Life is good when _____

My happiest memory is _____

My favorite school subject is _____ because I am good at _____

I feel best when _____

(Who) _____ encourages me most by _____

I like my life because _____

(Who) _____ makes me feel special because _____

I am most proud of _____

Life is good when _____

Unit 5:

SELF-ABSORBED

Slippery Momma

Mya is hoping to talk to Momma about the bully attack but Momma is so self-absorbed, she seems distant and uninterested. Mya befriends the landlord's cat, Meowy, who suffers similar problems. They are both leading a bullied life.

Lesson	Objectives	Student Goals	Materials and Lesson	Insights	Author's Message
Story #5 **Slippery Momma**	Students learn that Mya wishes to speak to Momma about the bully attack. Mya's desire to talk to Momma fails as Momma only shows concern for her tired feet. Students sympathize with Mya's plight.	Students understand Mya's rejection. Momma avoids her and directs Mya to make dinner. It is difficult to deal with this type of treatment. They see that Mya puts her needs aside and deals with her mother's wishes.	Students need a copy of the text. It can be read aloud to students, or they can read it silently. Small groups can also read together.	Mya's loneliness and isolation is clearly depicted in this section of the story. Her house was dark and locked. All that was left for her was a shovel to scoop up the cold, wet snow. It is a metaphor for what she faced and how she truly felt.	If we regard ourselves with unconditional personal acceptance, then we can extend that compassion to others. Perhaps Momma is experiencing a personal dislike for the person she has become. Her own inner conflict over single parenthood and a broken home must be occupying her thoughts.
Discussion Questions	These questions encourage students to explain why Mya felt sick when she lied to Mrs. Chinkley, why her relationship with Mrs. Chinkley was becoming closer, and how much she needed to be valued by someone.	Students understand Mya's needs. She needed to be loved, she needed to feel valued by someone, and she needed to be heard by a caring person. Her pain is revealed.	Students need the discussion questions and a copy of the text to look for the answers. There is an opportunity for open dialogue among students in the form of large group conversations.	We don't always take the time to listen to our family members when they are in need of comfort.	For Mya, Mrs. Chinkley took over Momma's role temporarily. Perhaps Mya understood that Momma was dealing with her own bigger problems at this time. Mya was patient enough to wait for her comforting words when the time was right.
Activity 1: **Summarize Your Best Qualities**	Students write a *Distinguished Student* paragraph, stating their abilities, successes, and accomplishments. They imagine that they have been selected for this honor and write a tribute to themselves listing their talents.	Students recall that they have value, talents, and abilities that they should be proud of.	Students need a pencil, a copy of the worksheet, and time to write a paragraph about their best qualities. Journaling about themselves helps them see their own value.	Self-acceptance and self-confidence is difficult for most of us to achieve. Listing our best qualities and reading them aloud, helps us realize our own value.	Seeing our goodness and accepting ourselves unconditionally is a very powerful experience. We must see ourselves for who we are, not for who we would like to be. This is revealing. It motivates us to feel compassion and acceptance for our talents and ourselves.
Activity 2: **Impression**	Students fill in a chart about the person who has impressed them the most. They discover that it is important to remember the special people in their lives.	Students scan their memories for events and people who treated them with kindness as Mrs. Chinkley did with Mya.	Students need the worksheet and pencil. They write down the name of a person who has made a big impression on them. Then they fill in boxes listing all the kindnesses extended by this person. Lastly, they add the feelings that the kindnesses brought about.	Writing out these memories of kind deeds makes a person appreciative of blessings others have brought to their lives.	Good deeds make a greater impression on us than do bad experiences. However, we mostly dwell on our failures and shortcomings. We must focus on the positives and forget the events and people that have hurt us.
Activity 3: **Impression Letter**	Students appreciate how important it is to write a thank you letter to someone who once impressed them by showing them kindness. It is important to think about how those actions impacted their lives.	Students practice putting feelings and thoughts on paper in order to value others' good deeds.	Students will need the worksheet, pencil, and time to write out this letter. Once finished, they make a copy and plan to hand deliver it to the person it concerns.	It is important to express gratitude to those who have helped us along our way.	Once we see that others extend kindnesses freely and without expectation of reward, we begin to do the same.
Activity 4: **Thankful**	Students recall all the people, events, and things in their lives that they are thankful for.	Students learn that it is important to appreciate the little things we often take for granted.	Students need a copy of the worksheet and a pencil. They will fill in the sheet with things that they are thankful for.	It is important to be glad for the people in our lives, for the things we love, and for the joyous experiences we have had.	When we begin to list all these things that we are thankful for, we are humbled by the amount of blessings we truly have.

SLIPPERY MOMMA

A bird-clock hung on the back wall in Chinkley's Produce Market. Mya heard it chirp three times. The red cardinal pointed to three o'clock. She knew she had about a half hour before she needed to head for home. She had been sweeping since she finished her hot chocolate and Mrs. Chinkley asked her to polish the apples that were knocked on the ground earlier that day. As she polished, she thought about getting home after a day that started out with great difficulty, but ended in sweetness.

Before she knew it, the clock peeped three thirty. It was the time school normally ended. Mya hoped Momma would be in a good mood so she could tell her about her eventful day. The snow had finally stopped. She put on her coat. Mrs. Chinkley came over and stuffed her pockets with apples and oranges and walked her to the door.

"Well Mya McGreggor, I am so glad you *ran* into us today," said Mrs. Chinkley with a twinkle in her eye and a chuckle in her voice. The wrinkles around her face seemed to show themselves more now. Mya knew what she meant and smiled at her weak attempt at making a joke.

Mrs. Chinkley added, "Take these pieces of fruit home to your Momma and if she wishes to call me tonight, I am giving you this card with my home number on it. Tell her not to hesitate to call. I'd like to tell her what a wonderful daughter she has but I am sure she already knows that." Then she slipped the card into Mya's pocket.

Mrs. Chinkley put her arm around Mya's small shoulders and gave her a squeeze. She said, "Now are you sure your momma will be home, Mya? Perhaps you should call first. You probably need to make sure your momma is home waiting for you."

Mya looked up at this kind, gray-haired woman. Some of her wispy hair fell down her cheek from across her forehead. She wasn't very big but her arm felt strong across Mya's back. Mya was drawn into her warm brown eyes and the crinkly smile. The lines surrounding her eyes looked like quotation marks. She knew she had found a special friend in Mrs. Chinkley.

Mya decided she couldn't call Momma. They couldn't afford a phone yet but she couldn't tell Mrs. Chinkley that. She was too embarrassed. She looked down at the floor and mumbled softly, "N-N-No, I-I-I know she will be home. She is expecting me and is probably making dinner right now." She couldn't look at Mrs. Chinkley while she lied.

Mya felt awful. She was the one who made dinner every night. Sometimes it was just peanut butter and banana sandwiches because she wasn't that good of a cook. She couldn't bear to tell Mrs. Chinkley that her mother hated cooking, made her daughter cook every night, and worried about herself more than she worried about her daughter. That was Momma's way. She was very fragile and Mya was the strong one in the family, or at least she had been, up until now.

As she walked out the door, she suddenly stopped, turned around, and ran back to hug Mrs. Chinkley really tight. When she realized what she'd done, she felt embarrassed about the hug and pulled away quick. Then she turned and ran as fast as she could toward Washington Boulevard.

Again she noticed tears welling up in her eyes, but this time she didn't know why. Nobody had been mean to her. In fact, it was just the opposite. Somebody had finally been nice to her. She held onto the fruit in her pockets to stop them from bopping against her hips while she ran. She hoped and prayed her mother would be home waiting for her when she arrived. She had so much to tell her.

But it was not to be because, when she got to number 32 Washington Boulevard, there wasn't a soul around. There was no car, no nothing. The house was all dark and cold looking. She noticed that the landlord, Mr. Blanko, or his son Bobby, had shoveled the sidewalk because there was less snow on the walkway than in the yard. The shovel leaned up against the doorframe. It was probably meant to remind someone else to keep up with the shoveling, so to stay warm, Mya began digging at the snow and ice. Mr. Blanko was a very unfriendly man, and she was truly surprised that the walk had been shoveled at all.

As she began scooping up the heavy wet snow, Mya felt as if someone was watching her. She turned around but saw nothing. She shrugged her shoulders and went back to her job. Her mind wandered to Franka and Bonnita. She secretly smiled when she thought about the day she stood up against them on the playground, and how Mrs. Chinkley saved her from their horrible snowball torture that afternoon.

Unfortunately, she knew the bullies would eventually make more trouble for her, but at the present moment, she didn't have to listen to them. They had been outsmarted two times and she knew they would not ever let Mya get away with that. She had finally made a new friend in this unfriendly town and that made her feel really good. However, at the moment, her only worry was clearing the walk before Momma got home.

Feeling someone's gaze again, she sensed it was coming from behind her. She peeked out of the corners of her eyes, slightly moving her head. She meant to see who was watching her but the only thing she noticed was Mr. Blanko's cat, Meowy, standing on the driveway behind her. Poor Meowy. She was a hated animal. The other morning, as Mya watch from her bedroom window, she saw Mr. Blanko try to kick at this lovely cat when she came near him. Mya thought back to the other night when a cat sat on her windowsill and blinked at her. She now realized it had been Meowy.

Mya wondered why the cat was named Meowy. She seemed so quiet. And more, she wondered why the man even had a cat when he hated her so much?

Meowy was very skittish. She ran under the porch as Mya tried to reach out to pet her. She was quite a pretty cat, kind of gray with bits of orange dotted all over and one white front paw. There was a patch under her chin that looked like a white triangle. Mya stared at the cat's beautiful eyes. Her lime green eyes seemed to hypnotize as they stared from under the porch.

Suddenly, a car pulled into the driveway. It was Momma. Mya dropped the shovel and ran toward the car. As she ran, the apples and oranges popped out of her pockets onto the snowy lawn. The look on Momma's face sent the girl a very negative message.

Momma slipped out of the car right passed her daughter. She never even saw the fallen fruit in the snow bank nor did she notice the shoveled snow. Momma was as quick as lightning. She slipped by Mya so fast that the girl couldn't keep up with her own mother.

As Mya reached out for a hello hug from Momma, the hurried woman was already at the front door jiggling the key in the lock. She yelled back at Mya, "You'd better get dinner started. I am too tired to cook tonight, Honey. Momma's been on her feet all day and they are just killing me. I am going to lie down for a bit. There's some ham and cheese in the fridge. I think we also have a can of tomato soup in the cupboard. Call me when it is ready." She entered the house and closed the door. Mya was left alone again.

Mya sadly finished shoveling and put the tool back up against the wall with a sigh. Momma wasn't the only one who had had a long hard day, thought Mya, but she knew she wouldn't be telling Momma about the events of her day at dinner.

From under the steps, two lime green eyes met Mya's. They blinked as if they knew how Mya felt right at that moment. Mya blinked back.

Slippery Momma

Discussion Questions

 Why did Mya feel sick when she lied to Mrs. Chinkley about Momma being home?

 Why did Mya run back and hug Mrs. Chinkley really tight before she left for home?

 Why did Mya feel tears well up in her eyes when she noticed someone finally being nice to her?

Summarize Your Best Qualities

Mya began to doubt her own value as she continued to run up against Franka and Bonnita. They terrorized and plotted against her to destroy her self-confidence. This activity could have helped her appreciate her self-worth. After completing it, she might have been strong enough to survive future attacks. Since she had no one to turn to, sitting down with herself and thinking about her value as a person may have helped her. She would begin to believe in herself and not accept what they said about her.

Imagine that you have been asked to be on a panel of *Distinguished Students* in your classroom. If the presenter were to introduce you, he or she would need a summary of your best qualities. In this activity, you will be asked to write a paragraph about yourself, filling it with all your wonderful talents. Here you will have a chance to write a summary about all the things you like about yourself.

Include and check off at least 5 of these items as you write your paragraph on the next page:

❏ Tell 3 things you like about your looks.

❏ Find the good things you like about two of your weakest traits and tell about them. (If you need help, refer to where Mya found goodness in her day of horrible events in Story #5.)

❏ Describe several things you can do well.

❏ Tell how daring you are to try new things.

❏ Remember the projects you have had success with. Describe them.

❏ Tell about things you would like to create.

❏ Write about what you would like to accomplish in your life.

❏ Describe what your friends like about you.

❏ Mention the 3 things you are most proud of. Tell why they make you proud.

❏ Tell about one thing you attempted and failed but never gave up trying. What made you want to go on?

❏ Remember to write your paragraph using good spelling and your proudest handwriting.

Now when your class has this type of presentation, the person describing you will have plenty of information about you to read to the audience.

MY BEST QUALITIES

_____

_____

_____

_____

_____

_____

_____

_____

_____

_____

_____

_____

_____

_____

_____

_____

_____

_____

_____

_____

_____

_____

_____

_____

_____

Big Impression

Think about Mrs. Chinkley. She made a big impression on Mya. She took her into the market, offered her hot chocolate and friendship, and made Mya feel safe. Mrs. Chinkley also took an interest in Mya's bully attack. She asked her questions and made her feel comfortable enough to talk about the events of the morning. In fact, Mrs. Chinkley made Mya feel so peaceful, she started to forget about the attack.

In this activity, you will recall a person who once treated you with kindness and acceptance. Remember the nice things this person did for you.

Here is your task:

- Think about a person who treated you with kindness in the past.

- In the box below, write the full name of the person who made the biggest impression on you.

- Think of all the nice things he or she did for you. Write them out.

- Then tell how these kindnesses made you feel.

Who Most Impressed You?	
Kindnesses	**How You Felt**
_____	_____
_____	_____
_____	_____
_____	_____
_____	_____
_____	_____
_____	_____

Big Impression Letter

ACTIVITY 3, STORY #5: SLIPPERY MOMMA

In the last activity you recalled the name of someone who impressed you most and wrote about the kindnesses that were extended to you. In this activity, your task will be to thank him/her for what was done. Use information from Activity #2 to complete this assignment.

Remember when Mya hugged Mrs. Chinkley as she left the market for home? She wasn't sure why she hugged the woman, but she knew it felt good. That hug was a thank you. It said, "Thank you for being kind to me when no one else was."

Your job for this activity is to:

- Write a letter to the person who was kind to you.
- Thank him or her for the good deeds extended to you.
- Write how the kindnesses made you feel.
- Use your best spelling and proudest handwriting.
- Decorate your paper with pictures or stickers.
- Be sure to end the letter with, "Thank you for your kindnesses."
- Deliver the letter personally.

Write your rough draft here before you transfer it to your stationery:

Dear _____ ,

_____

_____

_____

_____

_____

_____

With kind regards,

_____

Thankful List

ACTIVITY 4, STORY #5: SLIPPERY MOMMA

There are probably a lot of things and people you are thankful for. Mya was thankful for the concern Mrs. Chinkley showed her when she was at the market. She gave her hot chocolate, asked her about her family, gave her fruit to take home, and offered to talk with Momma about the events of the afternoon.

In this activity, your job will be to list things, events, and people that you are thankful for. Let your thoughts take you way back to your earliest memories. Share the ones you are most thankful for with your classmates.

Write your list on the next page.

Things, Events, and People I am Thankful For

EXAMPLE: I am thankful Dad talked me into getting back on when I fell off my horse.

I am thankful _____

I am thankful _____

I am thankful _____

I am thankful _____

I am thankful _____

I am thankful _____

I am thankful _____

I am thankful _____

I am thankful _____

I am thankful _____

I am thankful _____

I am thankful _____

I am thankful _____

I am thankful _____

I am thankful _____

I am thankful _____

I am thankful _____

I am thankful _____

I am thankful _____

I am thankful _____

I am thankful _____

I am thankful _____

I am thankful _____

I am thankful _____

I am thankful _____

I am thankful _____

Unit 6:

MYA'S FEARFUL DAY

STORY #6   SUMMARY

Reading Connections

Mya is faced with a fearful situation when Mrs. Braxton, her teacher, asks her to read her book report aloud. Her writing states her opinion on bullies and doesn't sound at all like the other students' reports. Feelings of unworthiness and self-doubt crop up.

Lesson	Objectives	Student Goals	Materials and Lesson	Insights	Author's Message
Story #6 **Reading Connections**	Students read about an incident in class when Mya feels so unsure of herself that she cannot make herself read a paper she wrote. Students see the control the bullies have over her. They see how the bullies have whittled away at her confidence.	Students identify with Mya's fear when she realizes that the students' reports sound very different from hers. They understand that reading her work aloud to the class is bound to result in more ridicule. There is a good reason why she shrinks from recognition.	Students need a copy of the text. It can be read aloud to students, or they can read it silently. Small groups can also read together.	Humiliation is very familiar to Mya and she can't take the chance of exposing herself to more of this treatment. She feels unworthy of any attention given to her by the teacher.	Mrs. Braxton, Mya's 5th grade teacher, is pleasantly surprised by the girl's writing ability. She is sensitive enough to go along with Mya and not expose her. Mya realizes that she thinks and writes differently from her classmates and is uncomfortable with being different.
Discussion Questions	These questions encourage students to explain why Mya identifies so deeply with the book on bullies. They imagine what Bonnita and Franka were thinking as Mya refused to read her assignment. They infer why Mrs. Braxton decided not to push Mya to read to the class.	Students gain an insight into Mya's thinking through her writing assignment. There is a foreshadowing about a change that begins to take place in Mya as she realizes she is different from her classmates. This difference may promise to be a good thing.	Students need the discussion questions and a copy of the text to look for the answers. There is an opportunity for open dialogue among students in the form of large group conversations.	We all must dare to be different because the differences we possess make us unique. We must show off our individuality. It makes us stand out. Most school age children do not accept this thinking. They feel it is good to be a copycat to fit in.	Differences are a cause for celebration, not a reason to cover up and withdraw. We must become less judgmental of others and ourselves and more tolerant of the differences that make us special. Let us celebrate differences instead of ridiculing them.
Activity 1: **Planning a Powerful Speech**	Students see that self-talk needs to be supportive and that we all need practice speaking in front of the class. This activity involves writing a speech to do just that.	Students are given suggestions on speech topics and a chart to plan a speech. They realize how negative self-talk may have stopped them from accomplishing something wonderful.	Students need the worksheet, pencil, and time to fill in the chart that helps them plan their speech.	Often we talk ourselves out of successfully accomplishing something because we feel inadequate and full of doubt. Fear takes over our thinking and we succumb to its spell.	Self-limiting doubts plagued Mya and dismantled her confidence. She concluded there were errors in her thinking so she put her classmates' abilities above her own when, in reality, she was the star.
Activity 2: **Writing a Powerful Speech**	Students learn the best way to compose a speech, include a powerful message, and improve it to make it easily presentable. They use the information charted in the previous activity to write a speech on a suggested topic.	Following an example, students write a speech and mark it with underlines to emphasize words that need to be spoken with strength.	Students need a copy of the worksheet, pencil, and time to work on their speechwriting. There are plenty of clues to direct students to make the best possible speech.	Speech writing can help students improve presentations in all subject areas.	Students must not be afraid to show their personalities in writing. Confidence grows as their work quality improves and the feedback becomes more and more positive and supportive.
Activity 3: **Delivering Your Speech**	Students are directed to practice reading over their speeches to become more and more confident. They use underlines to help them deliver the message strongly and carefully. Pointers are emphasized throughout the worksheet to make the speech memorable.	Students strive to demonstrate to their audience that their message is valuable and needs to be heard. Throughout their practice, they encourage themselves with positive self-talk. They prove their message is important by presenting with a loud confident voice.	Students need their speeches, time to practice at home or with small groups of classmates, and a day when all speeches are to be given in class. Inviting guests such as the principal, other classes, parents, and grandparents, will motivate students to deliver wonderful speeches.	Confidence comes when a person feels comfortable speaking in front of a large group.	Students always get nervous when standing in front of their peers to give a presentation. Their voices become softer, their eyes stare at the paper, and their words drone on and on. The message here is that they can be taught to become good presenters, and it is a valuable lesson for life.
Activity 4: **Grading Rubric for Speeches**	Students are graded on their speeches by using this rubric. It breaks down the requirements for a good speech into five parts. Students are judged on preparation and delivery. The speech is then assigned a value.	Students are motivated to work toward attaining the highest score possible. An advantage of using this rubric is that it will show them the areas they need to improve upon.	The teacher needs a copy of the rubric to score each speech-maker. She can use it when conferring with individuals about strengths and weaknesses. Peers can also use the rubric to score the speeches. Peer acceptance is important.	Sometimes we need to be evaluated, especially when we have practiced and practiced. Feeling confident about what we say has more value when our audience understands and agrees with the message.	It is good to see our weaknesses, our mistakes, and our errors. If we look at them as gifts to help us improve, we see them in a more positive light. We can then use them to grow from.

READING CONNECTIONS

School had been normal for four whole days. Franka was home sick with a bad cold and Bonnita acted just like any ordinary kid when Franka was absent. It seemed that when they were teamed up, they became mean. Mya was fine with Franka out of her life. She guessed Franka had caught a cold the day of the ambush. In Mya's mind, it served her right.

It was Friday and Mya congratulated herself for having a pleasant week. Unfortunately, the worst happened. Franka walked into the classroom just when Mya was reviewing her four peaceful days.

She quickly made herself busy getting her homework out for the day's lessons. Mya's most favorite school subject was reading. She loved losing herself in a book and often pretended she was living the life of the characters she read about. In class, however, she was very shy when it came to answering questions about the stories and characters. She was afraid to be wrong and she never volunteered answers. She didn't dare raise her hand in class, especially in this classroom. She knew some people would judge her based on her poor answers. She didn't feel very smart there.

That week, Mya and the class had been assigned to read a chapter book. A book report was due Friday. It was Friday and Mya was ready with her report. She pulled out her paper and felt some pride as she looked over her careful handwriting.

She had read the book easily and wrote her report early in the week. She was excited about this particular assignment because she wanted to tell her feelings about the main character, who just happened to be a mean bully. After all, she had a lot of experience with this subject.

She hated how the boy in the story treated everybody around him horribly. He especially loved to pick on younger kids.

She completed the book and the report in no time.

Writing was another one of her favorite subjects. Mya loved writing her thoughts on paper. It was so much easier than telling people how she felt. Writing down thoughts gave a person plenty of time to think through what to say and the reader could draw their own conclusions alone, without the writer being there.

Mya had a strong opinion about bullies. She thought that they enjoyed making others feel bad because they actually disliked their lives. They felt good when they made others feel awful. She thought the boy bully in the book might have been mistreated at home so he became a bully to get even with his parents and anyone he thought he could abuse. It was hinted that his dad gave him some trouble. She enjoyed the part where the bully got ambushed by a group of classmates who stood up to him. She ended her report with, "If I had my way, all bullies would get punished in real life, just like in this book."

That morning, Mrs. Braxton asked her students to be ready to read their reports aloud. Mya got scared when she heard this. She was very unsure of herself in front of this class. She was especially nervous about speaking to the two people who had made her feel bad about herself over the last few weeks. And considering what she said about bullies in her writing, she knew there was no way she was going to read what she wrote to the real bullies who sat behind her.

As Mrs. Braxton went around the room calling on students, each stood and read their piece to the class. Mya began to notice that the reports were all sounding the same. In fact they were becoming very boring because mostly the kids just retold the story from beginning to end. Mya's writing was totally different. She wove a little bit of the story into sentences about her thoughts and feelings that came from reading the book. She lived the story in her head all week long.

Of course, the next two to read were her playground enemies, Franka and Bonnita. They sat right behind her and when they each stood to read their uninspiring reports, Mya only felt herself dreading her turn more and more.

She believed that she had not followed the directions for the assignment. Her writing was like a report on bullying, and all the more reason to be worried about presenting it in front of the class. Suddenly, Mrs. Braxton called on her. "Mya, are you ready to share your report?" she asked.

Mya stared at her desk. She fiddled with her paper and quickly flipped it over. She sucked air and hardly breathed any out when she heard her name again. She searched for words to respond. She did not want to give the bullies another reason to attack and ridicule her.

"Mya, did you write a report for us today?" asked Mrs. Braxton. "Is that your report on your desk?"

Mya surprised herself and found some words to mumble under a tucked chin, but they were lies. She said, "N-N-N-O-O, Mrs. Braxton, I-I-I forgot all about it last night." She lied more, "This is just the beginning. I never finished it. I can't possibly read this. It sounds bad. Can I give up my recess and finish it then? I will hand it in later." She hated lying and saying her work wasn't done. Mya always finished her homework.

In her mind, she thought she'd rewrite it so it sounded like everybody else's. She didn't want her work to stand out and give her enemies a chance to laugh at her.

Behind her, she already heard a few nasty snickers. She knew where they were coming from but she refused to give them the satisfaction of turning around and letting the bullies know they were hurting her feelings again.

Mrs. Braxton shot a narrow-eyed look at the two girls sitting behind Mya and walked over to Mya's desk. She picked up Mya's paper saying, "May I?" She skimmed it over with her eyes not waiting for Mya's answer. "Why Mya," she said, "you did write a report, didn't you? Hmmm, let me read this over silently." Her eyes quickly read the piece and she looked up at Mya when she was finished.

Before Mya could open her mouth to say something to Mrs. Braxton about her writing, she heard some voices behind her whispering in a little song, "My-a's a li-ah, My-a's a li-ah, My-a's a li-ah!"

At that, the tears started to well up in her eyes and Mrs. Braxton fired the girls another look. She never noticed Mya's anguish. She was busy sending angry-eyed stares at Bonnita and then Franka. The voices stopped quite suddenly. Mya wiped her eyes with her sleeve without anyone noticing.

Mrs. Braxton looked at Mya and said, "Mya, your report seems to be finished and it looks quite interesting. Let me read it over again more carefully and I'll get back to you on it." Mrs. Braxton did notice that Mya's work was not at all like the others but it didn't seem to bother her. She threw a smile Mya's way. For some reason Mya was pleased at Mrs. Braxton's reaction.

As the teacher walked to her desk and placed the paper there, Mya felt a poke in her back. She saw herself getting smaller and smaller. She wished she could disappear because she knew what was coming. She heard the painful words seeming to pierce her heart as they were whispered in her ear, "Can't you do anything right? You aren't very smart." Then she heard the laughs.

Reading Connections

Discussion Questions

 Why did Mya think that the boy bully in the book she was reading probably was mistreated or abused at home?

 What were the bullies thinking about Mya as she told Mrs. Braxton that her report was incomplete?

 As Mrs. Braxton looked over Mya's report, she smiled at Mya. Mya enjoyed her reaction to the report. Imagine what Mrs. Braxton was thinking and discuss why she went along with Mya and allowed her to put off reading the report.

Planning a Powerful Speech

Mya was afraid to speak in front of her classmates because she was unsure of herself. First, she realized her writing was not anything like the reports her classmates read to the class. As she listened to their work, she noticed her writing didn't seem to fit the pattern theirs followed. She probably said to herself, "Mya, you can't read this. It sounds way too different. You didn't follow the directions."

Second, she knew Franka and Bonnita would ridicule her. Mya decided she'd pretend she was not finished so she wouldn't have to share her work with the class. She may have thought, "Mya, why read this to the class? You will only make Franka and Bonnita laugh at you and make you feel small. Don't do it. Just pretend you are not done so you can rewrite it to sound like the others."

Third, she felt that her work wasn't good enough to be read aloud. It was very different from the rest. She assumed it was no good. She thought it sounded ridiculous. She didn't think anyone would understand her message. She felt her work was wrong. She valued her classmates' writing above her own.

In this activity, you are going to plan a speech. Your speech will explain, through example, how a person's negative thoughts can result in failure.

If Mya wrote a speech about this incident, she could have written about the negative thoughts running through her mind as she convinced herself that her writing was not good enough to share with her classmates.

Here are some suggestions for your topic:

- Is there a job you were unable to finish properly because you didn't feel you could?
- Have you ever failed a test because you doubted your own thinking?
- Was there something you were unable to accomplish because you gave up on yourself?
- Has someone told you that you can't do anything right?
- Did you miss a ball and make an out for your team?
- Have you rolled a gutter ball when you intended to knock out ten pins?
- Were you ever last to be chosen for a team?
- Have you ever done something so poorly that it made you angry with yourself?
- What negative names have you called yourself because you failed at something you tried to do?
- What have the voices in your head said to remind you that you are not perfect enough.
- What negative statements and thoughts convinced you that you were not good enough?
- Tell how you once heard someone say corrosive words to you, and now you say them to yourself.
- Tell how negative talk makes you doubt your own abilities and skills.

There will be two parts to your speech.

- **Part 1** will be about the things you were not able to accomplish because of the corrosive talk you used to belittle yourself.

- **Part 2** will be about what you could have accomplished if you had a second chance. It will include examples of positive self-talk.

If Mya had the chance to prepare in this way, she probably would have stood up and read her report with pride in her voice. She would realize that she put thought and heart into her writing while the rest of the class just retold the story.

Planning Your Speech

Part 1: How were you unsuccessful?

Fill in the blanks with words and thoughts that explain the statements at the top of each column.

Tell what you were trying to accomplish.	What corrosive thoughts stopped you?	How did the cutting words make you feel?

Part 2: Plan for your second chance.

Fill in the blanks with words and thoughts that explain the statements at the top of each column.

How Would You Change Your Behavior?

What encouraging words will you now say to yourself?	How would these positive thoughts make you feel?	How would the outcome change?

Writing a Powerful Speech

 This activity will help you develop your speech in a powerful way. In the last activity, you planned it and in this activity, you will write it in preparation to present to your classmates.

Not only is the message of your speech important, but your delivery is too. The way you present a speech to your audience can be very moving. Phrasing impacts the listeners and can truly change their thinking. Remember, words have power and they can influence peoples' minds. You want your listeners to get your message. They need to understand how doubting words stopped you from accomplishing something you have always regretted. They must also hear how your self-talk has become kinder.

If you watch someone giving a speech, you'll notice the speaker emphasizes certain words by saying them louder and pauses to let the message sink in. The speechmaker may even use hand gestures to emphasize a point.

Once you have written your speech, go back and reread it. Use a pencil to underline one important word in each sentence. This will help with your delivery. Later when you give your speech, you will say these underlined words with a much stronger voice to emphasize their importance.

An example of a speech is on the next page. The underlined words are the ones that would be spoken with a stronger voice. Try to read it aloud giving strength to the words that are underlined. Notice how this process gives the speech more meaning and keeps your attention.

Why I Don't <u>Ever</u> Sing

When I was about four years old, I <u>loved</u> singing around the house. I sang in the <u>shower</u>, I sang in my bedroom, and I even sang around the kitchen. Then my big brother said, "<u>Stop singing!</u> I can't <u>stand</u> it. Your voice <u>stinks</u>. You sound like a cow <u>bellowing</u> in the fields."

His words <u>hurt</u> me in a very bad way! They made me feel <u>embarrassed</u> and self-conscious about my voice. I just wanted to run to my room and <u>hide</u>, so I did.

I <u>believed</u> what he said about my voice so I stopped singing. From that day on, I <u>never</u> sang when people were around, ever again. I <u>missed</u> singing, but I wouldn't sing because I was sure everybody just heard bellowing.

Then I went to <u>kindergarten</u>. The <u>music</u> teacher asked me to sing. I was <u>afraid</u> but I sang just a little. She told me my voice was <u>great</u>. I <u>knew</u> she was wrong. My brother was <u>older</u> and smarter than me. In <u>my</u> mind he knew just about everything. When he told me I bellowed, I <u>knew</u> he had told me the truth. I <u>believed</u> him above everyone. His words kept haunting me "<u>Stop</u> singing. I can't <u>stand</u> it. Your voice <u>stinks!</u> You sound like a cow <u>bellowing</u> in the fields."

I chose <u>not</u> to sing that year. I <u>hated</u> what he said but I believed it. If I could <u>change</u> what happened, I'd have him say, "I <u>love</u> your voice! It sounds like birds singing on a <u>spring</u> morning. Don't ever stop, <u>please</u>." These kind words make me feel <u>good</u> about my voice.

I have decided to say <u>these</u> words to myself every time I feel like singing. I am beginning to <u>like</u> to sing again. I realize he was <u>wrong</u>. I <u>do</u> have a pretty good voice. And the more I sing, the more I <u>like</u> my voice.

■ Now write your speech on your own paper.
■ Remember to reread it and underline the strongest word in each sentence.

Delivering Your Speech

 Now it is time to practice your speech for presentation. Your goal will be to sound like a professional. A good trick for developing confidence is to practice, practice, and practice more. Plan to read your speech loudly and as much as possible.

Mya should have done this with her report. She would never have been embarrassed to share her work if she had thought of it like a speech. Speeches are read slower than normal talking. This is so that the audience understands and can think about the message.

Here are some tips for reading your speech:

- Always remember to look up at your audience to make eye contact.

- As you read over your speech, look for the underlined words and announce them loudly and clearly. Read slowly and carefully. Enunciate or pronounce your words clearly and thoroughly. You want your audience to pay close attention and understand your message. Remember, minds wander when they can't hear or make out what the speaker is saying.

- Good speechmakers repeat important phrases a few times to get their point across. While you are revising, find one powerful phrase. Rewrite it in your speech to emphasize your point to the audience.

- One of the weakest areas of a presentation is the volume of the speaker. Often, when kids feel fearful of talking in front of the class, they look down and speak so softly no one can hear them. They mumble like Mya, under their breath. They probably don't want anyone to hear them because they hate being the center of attention. Don't be one of those softies. Speak up! Be proud of what you think. It just may change people's minds and improve what they say to each other.

- Practice your speech by reading it over several times. Make sure it sounds like you are talking to someone when you read it. Practice in front of your family. Practice by yourself in front of a mirror.

- Be supportive and tell yourself how great you sound. Talk to yourself like you talk to your dog or cat. Say, "What a good speech. Oh, I love what I just said. It sounds so powerful!" Talking to yourself using kind words will give you confidence. Be ready to give your speech in a prideful way.

- Be bold when delivering your speech. Your speech will change the way your classmates talk to each other. They will begin to think about how words can hurt someone or can soothe a heart and make it sing. Words can change the world. Words have power.

- Celebrate the speeches on a special day in the classroom. Be ready to deliver your speech. Set up a podium and arrange the chairs like an audience. Invite other classes in to hear these speeches. Call in parents and the principal. They need to hear these messages, too!

Grading Rubric for Speeches

ACTIVITY 4, STORY #6: *READING CONNECTIONS*

To make sure your message is powerful and your delivery is memorable, it is important to have your speech scored. Below is a rubric to rate each part of the speech as it is being given. The teacher and students can use this as a grading chart. Teachers will use it to confer with students about the quality of their work. Students will score their peers as they listen to the speeches. Then the form will be cut up, passed to the speechmakers, and used as a way for students to see their strengths and weaknesses.

Each subdivision is worth a total of 20 points:

4 pts. = Weak

8 pts. = Try Harder

12 pts. = Average

16 pts. = Good

20 pts. = Fabulous

Total the points.
If speeches are perfectly presented,
students can achieve 100 points or 100%.

You can do it!

Grading Speeches

Name_____	Name_____	Name_____	Name_____
Planning:	Planning:	Planning:	Planning:
Enunciation:	Enunciation:	Enunciation:	Enunciation:
Volume:	Volume:	Volume:	Volume:
Delivery:	Delivery:	Delivery:	Delivery:
Message:	Message:	Message:	Message:
Total:	Total:	Total:	Total:
Name_____	Name_____	Name_____	Name_____
Planning:	Planning:	Planning:	Planning:
Enunciation:	Enunciation:	Enunciation:	Enunciation:
Volume:	Volume:	Volume:	Volume:
Delivery:	Delivery:	Delivery:	Delivery:
Message:	Message:	Message:	Message:
Total:	Total:	Total:	Total:
Name_____	Name_____	Name_____	Name_____
Planning:	Planning:	Planning:	Planning:
Enunciation:	Enunciation:	Enunciation:	Enunciation:
Volume:	Volume:	Volume:	Volume:
Delivery:	Delivery:	Delivery:	Delivery:
Message:	Message:	Message:	Message:
Total:	Total:	Total:	Total:
Name_____	Name_____	Name_____	Name_____
Planning:	Planning:	Planning:	Planning:
Enunciation:	Enunciation:	Enunciation:	Enunciation:
Volume:	Volume:	Volume:	Volume:
Delivery:	Delivery:	Delivery:	Delivery:
Message:	Message:	Message:	Message:
Total:	Total:	Total:	Total:
Name_____	Name_____	Name_____	Name_____
Planning:	Planning:	Planning:	Planning:
Enunciation:	Enunciation:	Enunciation:	Enunciation:
Volume:	Volume:	Volume:	Volume:
Delivery:	Delivery:	Delivery:	Delivery:
Message:	Message:	Message:	Message:
Total:	Total:	Total:	Total:

Unit 7:

EVERYONE DEALS WITH BULLIES

STORY #7 SUMMARY

On the Job at Chinkley's

Mya grows to love her job at Chinkley's. She and Mrs. Chinkley become the best of friends and the bond between them grows stronger and stronger. They have a serious discussion about a bully Mrs. Chinkley had past dealings with. The town bully, Mr. Calhoon, swindled her own father out of his fruit farm when she was a young girl. They bond even more with this connection.

Lesson	Objectives	Student Goals	Materials and Lesson	Insights	Author's Message
Story #7 **On the Job at Chinkley's**	Students read about a revealing conversation Mya and Mrs. Chinkley have regarding bullies. They conclude that Mrs. Chinkley has a good reason to help Mya fight off the bullies in her life.	Students find that Mrs. Chinkley is a smart woman. She shares her pointers about dealing with bullies in a clever way. They realize, as Mya does, that it is important not to give one's power away to bullies. It is wise to remain strong and steadfast.	Students need a copy of the text. It can be read aloud to students, or they can read it silently. Small groups can also read together.	The line, "My daddy died from a broken heart, broken by a bully," gave Mya inspiration. It was then that she realized something very important. Bullies take our power away from us and use it against us. They take joy in making fools of us.	Bullies turn a per strength into wea They take this stre and they use it ag their victims. Bul cause people to abandon themsel and side with the enemy. They attac and make people they deserve it. T cannot be allowe
Discussion Questions	These questions encourage students to analyze why Mrs. Chinkley's father would so easily give up his farm to a bully, what it means to give up one's power, and the message behind Mrs. Chinkley's bully story.	Students realize that Mrs. Chinkley truly plays a big role in Mya's life through her compassion, her gentle spirit, and her guided support. They come to understand that her unconditional acceptance of Mya helps the girl change.	Students need the discussion questions and a copy of the text to look for the answers. There is an opportunity for open dialogue among students in the form of large group conversations.	This chapter is a turning point in Mya's life. It begins her path of self-discovery and determination. She realizes she's better than her bullies, better than Momma thinks she is, and better than she herself believes she is.	Mrs. Chinkley cha Mya's life and ma her believe in her and realize that sh value. She shows that people can le from life's experie or be defeated by
Activity 1: **Dream Escape**	Students focus on their dreams. They envision the places they dream about as they escape from everyday issues. They discover that dreams can be sanctuaries to help us escape from reality. Mya was able to escape to a real-life sanctuary at Chinkley's Produce Market.	Students read about a boy named Max, who used a *Dream Escape* to separate himself from the issue of poverty. Being poor stopped him from owning a pony. He escaped reality each night as he created an imaginary escape in his mind. Students then sequence their imaginings.	Students need a pencil, a copy of the worksheet, and time to fill in the list. They describe, in sequence, the events that take place in their escape.	Often we have a need to escape from the stresses of our lives. We find ways to distract ourselves. Daydreaming is one way. Dreaming settles the mind, calms worries, and allows the person to go inward and discover a sense of peace.	Mya found a san at the produce m with Mrs. Chinkl She used it to for her troubles and good about herse We all need a sanctuary, if only our imaginations
Activity 2: **The Senses**	Students use a chart to describe the sensory images found in their dream.	Students bring their sanctuary into reality by imagining what they see, hear, smell, and feel. They chart these along with feelings they experience while in their escape.	Students need the worksheet and a pencil to jot down 5 examples for each of the sensory experiences in their escape.	Using a sensory approach to describe dreams brings their vividness to life. It is easier to visualize the journeys using sensory images. There is a greater chance to find peace when traveling there.	We experience lif through our sense why not in our dr
Activity 3: **Draw It**	Students create a sanctuary on paper by cutting, drawing, and coloring it.	Students' detailed drawings make their escapes seem more real and therefore emotionally inviting.	Students need the worksheet, a pencil, crayons, construction paper, markers, glue, and magazines. Once the materials are gathered, students cut and paste, draw, and color the escape on 12x18 paper.	Mya found peace at Chinkley's and it became a place she loved to go each day to escape. To her it was not just a job. To her it was a place to find herself. We all need something similar.	Students describe sanctuaries with detail and joy. Designing an esc reinforces individ and creativity. As Mrs. Chinkley wa Mya's encouragin so, too, students wish to include a person or a friend whose picture ma included in the e
Activity 4: **Write About It**	Students journey to their escapes through writing.	Students use the information from Activities 1-3 to describe a trip to their sanctuaries. It becomes an inviting place to go to when things worry them.	Students need the worksheet, a pencil, and time to write down their journey. The description and the drawings then go home to be hung on their bedroom wall. They can then be used for future trips.	There is comfort in the knowledge that all will be taken care of easily and quickly. The message here is that worrying is not the answer.	We often burden selves with probl We worry oursel over them rather doing something them. Worrying i tactic. It only cau more problems ir long run. Someti taking a peaceful escape calms ou enough to discov answers.

ON THE JOB AT CHINKLEY'S

Mrs. Chinkley was the first and only adult in town that treated Mya with respect. Each day before she started work, there was a cup of hot chocolate waiting for her on the back table. Mya loved working at the market after school and the more she worked, the more she enjoyed it.

She swept floors mostly, but sometimes, stacked fruit, put new prices up, and made colorful advertising signs for the windows. Mrs. Chinkley said Mya's spelling was perfect and her handwriting was so big and clear, everybody could read it. Mrs. Chinkley's writing was sloppy because she was always in a hurry when writing. People never seemed to be able to read it. They were always asking about the price when it was right in front of them.

Mya loved talking to Mrs. Chinkley. They were becoming good friends. Mrs. Chinkley seemed to understand Mya. It was as if she could read her mind about things. Mya got the feeling Mrs. Chinkley had some of the same experiences that Mya was facing.

One day Mya asked Mrs. Chinkley what she thought about bullies. Mrs. Chinkley slammed down her basket of bananas and hurried over to where Mya was sweeping. "Bullies? Bullies?" she asked. "What do I think about bullies? Why there is no place in this world for bullies. They should all be put together in their own city so they can spend their lives bullying each other instead of the rest of us."

She went on, "I had the misfortune of being bullied when I was a little girl. Actually my whole family was bullied. The Chinkley's were poor fruit farmers and we got our share of being bullied by the biggest bully in our town, Mr. Calhoon." There was a far away look in her eyes. Mya could see that Louise Chinkley knew personally how bullies could destroy a person's confidence.

"My daddy had a fruit farm and all seven kids worked hard helping him grow apples, peaches, plums, and pears. My brothers and sisters and I were out there picking, planting, plowing, or pruning everyday, right along with Daddy.

We grew fruit for the local markets and were proud of our harvest. Daddy knew how to protect the fruits from bugs, without using poisons, so our fruit was in big demand. Daddy bought the land with just a few thousand dollars when he was a young man, before he married my momma. When the kids came along, we helped it grow into a healthy orchard that sold tons of good fruit to the local customers.

Daddy was so proud of his business that he thanked us everyday for helping him farm the fruit. Everything I learned about fruit, I learned from my Daddy," she said proudly.

"Then one day, a rich man named Mr. Calhoon, came to the farm and offered Daddy seventy-five thousand dollars to take the farm off his hands.

The farm was worth a lot more but Mr. Calhoon was good at twisting words and changing peoples' beliefs! He made Daddy feel small by telling him he wasn't that good of a fruit farmer. He shamed him by saying he had to use his kids as fruit pickers instead of hiring people to work. He called him a poor man who couldn't even afford to have hired help to run his orchard.

Daddy got very sad when he heard that. He never thought it was a bad thing to use his kids to work the trees. He never thought of himself as a poor man. But when Mr. Calhoon said Daddy was stopping us from getting a good education, something changed in Daddy. He felt ashamed for making us work in the orchards instead of encouraging us go to college. Daddy felt awful. He started to feel he was a bad father to keep us from becoming something special," she told Mya.

She explained how Mr. Calhoon picked on her daddy over and over again, never letting up. He made it a point to visit everyday just to belittle him. Then there was a mysterious fire at her farmhouse in the middle of the night and that really scared her daddy. Everybody got out of the house in time but her father was never the same after that.

She said with a sad tone in her voice, "When Mr. Calhoon came around after the fire, he twisted Daddy's thoughts around until he wore him down. He made him feel worthless by telling him he was a poor man who made money off of his kids. He threatened that the next time there was a fire, we might not get out of the house safely. That did it. Daddy gave up the land. No one ever suspected that Mr. Calhoon had started the fire, but Daddy did. He never told anybody for fear of another one."

Mya looked in Mrs. Chinkley's teary eyes. There was a sadness there that she had never seen. Mrs. Chinkley turned away so Mya couldn't see the tear drop down her cheek. She said with her back to Mya, "Mr. Calhoon put a shopping mall where the peaches and apples once grew, and that money was nothing to a man like Calhoon.

What was even worse, he made Daddy feel like a failure and he was never the same after that. He went to work in a factory and hated being inside a dark building doing the same thing every day. Then one day, about two years later, he got sick and died. My daddy died from a broken heart, broken by a bully."

Mrs. Chinkley turned toward Mya and said, "I learned about bullies from Mr. Calhoon, the biggest and worst bully I have ever met. I will never let another bully push me or my friends around ever again." Then she paused for a moment and looked straight into Mya's eyes and said, "Mya, if you never remember anything else I have said to you, remember this, bullies may change a moment in your life. They may bring about a situation you never wanted or expected, but they don't ever have to change who you are! Don't give them your power."

Mya thought hard about that story. She pictured the fear in the eyes of the Chinkley children and the parents when their farmhouse was on fire. She imagined the smile on Mr. Calhoon's face when he handed Mr. Chinkley the check. The farm was worth much more than what he paid. She saw in her mind's eye, Mrs. Chinkley's daddy, a heartbroken man, who died from trying to do the best for his family. She decided she would be just like Mrs. Chinkley. Bullies, watch out!

Discussion Questions

 Bullies can damage peoples' lives, once they know they can. They become controlling and hungry with power. Explain how the bully, Mr. Calhoon, was able cause Mrs. Chinkley's father to sell his fruit farm even though he did not want to.

 What did Mrs. Chinkley mean when she said, "Bullies don't have to change who you are? Don't give them your power."

 Mya learned something very valuable from Mrs. Chinkley that day. It was more than just how to deal with bullies. What other knowledge did she gain?

Dream Escape

ACTIVITY 1, STORY #7: ON THE JOB AT CHINKLEY'S

Mya had a safe place to go after school everyday. She was a lucky girl. Chinkley's Produce Market was a haven from the bullies. She felt loved and needed there. She felt free enough to talk to Mrs. Chinkley about things that bothered her. We don't all have a safe haven to go to when we are scared but we do have our dreams.

When you are all by yourself with no one else around, do you dream about something you would love to experience? Do you use your daydreams to escape from the real world around you? *Dream Escapes* are good for your well-being. Mya had a real dream place to go to so she could forget the bullies for a while. She was lucky.

This is Max's Dream Escape:

Max Washington closed his eyes each night and dreamed the same dream. He imagined he had his own pony. But it was not the kind of pony he saw at the fairgrounds each summer. In his mind, Max created a mechanical, wind-up pony. He pretended to reach under his bed where Gogo, the pony, stayed during the day. Max pictured Gogo all in pieces so the horse could fit beneath the bed. He imagined that the animal was about the size of a real pony when he was all put together. When Gogo stood by the bed, Max imagined himself climbing on. He would wind the horse up with a key that would make the pony come to life.

Max invented Gogo because his dad said over and over that the family could never afford a real pony. His dad would tell him, "Max, you know you can't have a pony. We have nowhere to put it, we live in a city apartment, and we can't afford one anyway. We will never afford one. When you grow up and make a lot of money, buy one for yourself."

So Max did the next best thing. He created a pony in his imagination. Gogo had a bronze-colored coat and a black mane. His hoofs and legs were as white as his brother's tall basketball socks. Max loved to imagine the horse whinnying. When he was on Gogo's back, they'd go galloping all around his bedroom. The last thing they'd do is jump over the bed and out the window to the street below. The two of them would float gently to the ground. Max imagined a field of green, sweet smelling grass instead of a sidewalk. Gogo would put his head down first thing, to get a belly full of grass. He'd snort and crunch the grass and Max could tell by Gogo's reaction that it tasted good. Max could see the green grass sticking out of the pony's mouth as he chewed. Then they'd go zooming down the street, lickety-split.

Max was so happy when he was riding Gogo. He felt like he was flying around on a cloud. He loved dreaming about having a horse. He promised himself to one day have a real Gogo on his ranch when he grew up. Until then, he forgot all his worries and fears as he rode Gogo in his dreams. Each night riding Gogo made Max feel so peaceful he fell into a deep quiet sleep.

Think about your escape. Do you play every position on your own baseball team? You may drive racecars or get hired to play an important part in a movie. No matter what your dream is, it is good to have one. The important thing is that it makes you feel peaceful and it allows you to forget your worries.

Next to the numbers below, list in order, 5 events that take place in your *Dream Escape*.

1. _____

2. _____

3. _____

4. _____

5. _____

The Senses

When Mya entered the market, she noticed the fruity smells that bombarded her nostrils. When she heard her boss's gentle voice welcome her to work, she felt a sense of peace come over her. She could see Mrs. Chinkley's kind face greeting her from behind the counter. As she drank her cocoa, she'd swirl it all around her mouth first. Then, as she swallowed, she felt the chocolate coat her throat and stomach with its comforting warmth. She'd feel the broom brushing against the floor as she swept.

These sensory descriptions all helped Mya leave her troubles behind. As she did her job each day, she let go of the worried feelings she had.

On the lines below, list the things your senses notice in your Dream Escape.

Describe What Your Senses Experience

Name 5 things you see in your dream.

_____

_____

Name 5 things you hear in your dream.

_____

_____

Name 5 things you feel or sense in your dream.

_____

_____

Name 5 things you smell in your dream.

_____

_____

Name 5 feelings you experience in your dream. (Example: happiness, confidence, etc.)

_____

_____

Draw It

ACTIVITY 3, STORY #7: *ON THE JOB AT CHINKLEY'S*

In this activity you will bring your *Dream Escape* to life. Just as Mya could experience her escape each day after school, you will be creating yours on a sheet of construction paper. Using your list of details from Activity 1 and your sensory descriptions from Activity 2, draw your escape on a piece of 12x18 paper.

Here is your task. Be sure to:

■ Add lots of detail. The more details you add, the easier it will be to imagine as you take your journey. Your detailed imagination will help you find peace each time you visit.

■ It is good to have special people in your escape. Just as Mya had Mrs. Chinkley, you may wish to have someone there who welcomes you when you feel especially troubled. Paste or draw in a picture of this person, animal, or creature.

■ Perhaps you'll choose to make a collage rather than a drawing. Collect pictures from magazines to use in your collage. You may also add drawings to your collage.

■ When you finish, hang the picture on your bedroom wall at home to escape whenever you need to.

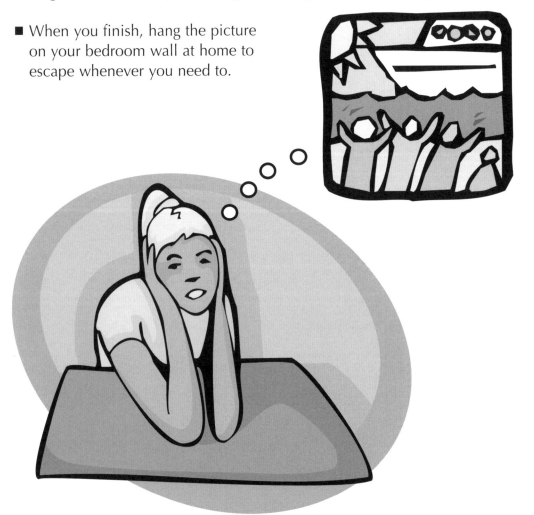

Write About It

All the lovely familiar things at Chinkley's Produce Market were just what Mya needed to separate herself from her troubles at school and home.

For this activity, your job will be to write out your Dream Escape experience. Try to detail these things:

- As you describe your escape in words, tell what you see, hear, feel, and smell. Use information from Activities 2 and 3.

- Use Max Washington's model to guide you.

- Tell about anyone who is there to greet and comfort you. Write down what they say or do to make you feel safe.

- Be sure to add the feelings you experience. Remember how peaceful Mya felt while at the market?

- When you finish, check your spelling and then copy it over on fresh paper in your proudest handwriting.

- Take it home and put it next to your drawing.

- Rough draft describing your *Dream Escape:*

_____

_____

_____

_____

_____

_____

_____

Unit 8:

THE BIG LIE

STORY #8 SUMMARY

Mrs. Chinkley Has Something up Her Sleeve

Mrs. Chinkley and Mya are surprised to find Franka Martin in the market one day. This leads to a devilish intervention by Mrs. Chinkley as she catches the girl in a big lie. She proves to Mya that her friendship is true.

on	Objectives	Student Goals	Materials and Lesson	Insights	Author's Message
#8 *Chinkley* *thing* *der* *e*	Students read about Mrs. Chinkley's intervention to stop Franka Martin from trying to take Mya's job at the Market. They appreciate her cleverness as she stops the girl. They see the woman as an ally who knows more about Mya than Mya thinks.	Students identify with Mya's anger as she recognizes Franka's motives in an attempt to demean Mya again. Luckily, Mrs. Chinkley proves her hunch about the girl is correct. She destroys the girl's lie. Students appreciate the woman's loyalty as she bolsters Mya's confidence with her little trick.	Students need a copy of the text. It can be read aloud to students, or they can read it silently. Small groups can also read together.	Mrs. Chinkley is a clever woman who has had experiences with bullies. She saw how careful Mya had been not to burden her with problems. She read between the lines.	Children must realize that it is a good thing to have a mentor to confide in. Mya was not used to trusting. Mrs. Chinkley had to prove to the girl that she was trustworthy and that it was safe to share knowledge with her.
ussion tions	These questions ask students to think about why Mrs. Chinkley threw a coughing fit, why the woman wanted to deal with the bully alone, and why she pretended to know the teacher, Mrs. Braxton.	Students attempt to reason why Mrs. Chinkley understood very well what Franka was up to. They decide why she cleverly squelched Franka without allowing Mya to say a word.	Students need the discussion questions and a copy of the text to look for the answers. There is an opportunity for open dialogue among students in the form of large group conversations.	Mrs. Chinkley pretended that she knew Mrs. Braxton. It was just a bluff. Was it wrong to trick the bully in this way? Perhaps she learned something from Mr. Calhoon. He might be shocked that he taught her.	Sometimes we have to beat the bullies at their own game. It shows our strength. It encourages our power to bubble up to the surface. It reminds the bully that we are not to be abused.
ity 1: ance	Students recall old memories, unhappy experiences, and sad times. Once they have drawn them and added thought bubbles, they release the memories by erasing them.	The action involved in drawing the incidents and then erasing shows students that past moments have little power in the present. They are only memories and they can be forgotten. Their minds will be free of negative, controlling worries.	Students need a pencil with an eraser, a copy of the worksheet, and time to draw the memories. As part of the experience, the class will have a ceremony to let go of these negative thoughts.	Choosing to let go of worrisome thoughts is empowering.	Joy and light-heartedness is healing to the spirit. Letting go of dark thoughts allows the light in.
ity 2: -Proof	Students learn how to deflect the criticisms of bullies. Sometimes a joke or a laugh breaks the seriousness of the moment and catches the bully off guard.	Students realize that there is often a need to laugh and that laughter is a behavior that can break the seriousness of a situation.	Students need the worksheet and a pencil. They also need a joke book to find jokes to memorize. They write the jokes around the drawing of a bully-proof vest. Once the jokes are memorized, they can be used to catch the bully off guard with laughter.	When moments get too serious and joy is the last thing on our minds, it is actually the perfect time to bring joy to the forefront and have a little laugh.	Students realize that joking is fun and light-hearted enough to ease the seriousness of any situation. It makes even the saddest, most frustrating moment seem small. There is joy in seeing the silver lining of any cloud.
ity 3: Sides	Students realize that every situation has two points of view. They see the advantages of being a bully and the disadvantages of being bullied.	Students see the bully's side as well as their own as they fill in a chart listing the pros and cons of bullying.	Students need the worksheet, a pencil, and time to fill in the chart. They begin to understand what bullies actually get out of bullying. They look at things from a bully's point of view.	Looking at the way a bully thinks and what motivates bullying behavior can actually have a good effect on the one who is bullied.	Bullies are at an advantage most of the time, but if the bullied person can see through the eyes of a bully, then he or she can anticipate ways to avoid unhappy situations.
ity 4: ing er	Students feel in control of situations by writing a persuasive argument against bullying. They use the information written on the *Bullying Chart*, from the previous activity.	Through this essay, students gain a new understanding of the viciousness of bullying and the controlling effect it has on the bullied person. They make strong arguments against bullying to convince bullies to end their tyranny once and for all.	Students need a copy of the directions for this activity, which includes an example of an essay on a related topic. The anti-bullying essays will be read as a class activity.	It is time to argue against the cruelties of bullying and stop its growth in our schools and media.	If students can present well thought out arguments against bullying, then perhaps future bullies will be deterred.

MRS. CHINKLEY HAS SOMETHING UP HER SLEEVE

One Friday afternoon at Chinkley's Produce Market, Mya was sweeping dust out from under the back counter. She had been mindlessly pushing the broom around, cleaning up the dirt, and humming a soft tune to herself. Her mind wandered to thoughts about sleeping in on Saturday morning. Suddenly, a voice caught her attention. It was a very familiar voice.

She turned around and looked to see who was speaking to Mrs. Chinkley. The girl had her back towards Mya. She was facing Mrs. Chinkley and they were standing by the display of oranges near the front window. As Mya continued sweeping, she noticed the girl asking Mrs. Chinkley something about the market.

Mya looked at the girl's head. She saw something very familiar. It was the wooly ski cap that jogged her memory. Some wavy, brown hair stuck out from under it. Suddenly, Mya's face tightened as she realized whose back she was staring at. Her jaw dropped when she heard the girl asking for her job. "Why that brat," thought Mya. "She has some nerve!"

Mya started to walk over to where the two were talking but suddenly noticed Mrs. Chinkley violently begin to cough. It sounded serious. As the girl in the ski hat reached to bang on Mrs. Chinkley's back to stop her cough, Mrs. Chinkley made a motion toward Mya.

Mrs. Chinkley had seen the rage in Mya's eyes when she saw who was asking about a job. She also remembered the conversation she and Mya recently had about bullies. Mrs. Chinkley cleverly connected these things with the day Mya had run into the apple crate. She intelligently came to the correct conclusion.

With her left hand on her throat and her eyes bulging, Mrs. Chinkley coughed uncontrollably while flicking her right hand several times. She was motioning Mya to go back. The signal was out of the girl's sight and it was a good thing because Mya was ready to use her broom for something other than sweeping.

"Are you all right?" asked the girl. She kept hitting Mrs. Chinkley's back, trying to get her to stop coughing. She had a worried look on her face and said, "You are such an old woman. You are not going to die are you?" At those words, Mrs. Chinkley almost wished she had the broom in her hands.

Mya turned around with the broom. She was squeezing it so tightly that her fingers turned white. She went by the back counter, pretending to sweep a different part of the store. She made it look like she was not really listening to the conversation when, in fact, she heard every nasty word.

Mrs. Chinkley abruptly finished coughing as soon as she saw Mya back by the hot chocolate table. As she eyed Mya over in the far corner, sweeping very slowly, she decided to play along with the girl to find out what was behind this sudden interest in a job. Mrs. Chinkley knew something fishy was going on. She asked, "So, Deary, what is your name?"

The girl answered, "Franka Martin."

Mrs. Chinkley continued, "What made you think I was looking for a new helper, Franka?"

As she watched Mrs. Chinkley continue with the job interview, Mya suddenly realized that this very special woman knew more about the stranger than she had previously thought. There must be something else up her sleeve other than her arm.

Franka answered, "Well, Mrs. Braxton, my teacher, was complaining in school today. She said that Mya McGreggor hasn't been getting her homework done like she used to. So I thought, maybe you need a helper who can sweep and get her homework done." Her eyes glanced over toward Mya. She had a tiny smile coming to the corner of her mouth, out of Mrs. Chinkley's sight, of course. She went on and pointed toward Mya, "I think you should send her home to do her homework." She said this in such a mean-spirited voice that Mya's eyes began to tear up.

She realized it was payback time. Franka was back to her bullying self again. She glared at Franka. Franka Martin had reached an all time low, telling lies. Mrs. Braxton never said any such thing to Mya at school that day, but how was Mrs. Chinkley to know the truth? She didn't even know Mrs. Braxton, or so Mya thought.

Mrs. Chinkley furrowed her eyebrows and started walking away from Franka. The girl looked puzzled but she followed the storekeeper over to the counter. She watched Mrs. Chinkley reach for the phone.

Mrs. Chinkley checked her watch and said, "Why it's not that late. She'll probably still be there. She often stays after to get her work done. "

"Who," asked Franka? "Didn't you even hear what I said? I want this job, so fire her. Hire me right now!"

Mrs. Chinkley seemed totally unaware of the bully's orders as she fumbled through a small black book for a phone number. Then she began pressing buttons. "I know Laura very well," she said. "In fact we just had coffee together last weekend. She is such a sweet person." She clicked her fingers on the counter.

"Laura who? Who are you talking about? Didn't you hear me? What about the job? Why aren't you asking me about my experience?" the girl asked.

"Shh, it's ringing," she said to Franka as she put her finger up to her lips.

All this time, Mya was doing all she could not to interfere. She so wanted to go over to Franka and bop her one. She felt so much stronger when she was around Mrs. Chinkley.

"Hello, Laura?" Mrs. Chinkley said. "I have a student here whose name is Franka Martin. She says she is in your class. She came to my store today with some mean gossip about a student in your class named Mya McGreggor."

Before Mrs. Chinkley could say another word, Franka bolted out the door with a very frightened look on her face. Mrs. Chinkley put down the phone after she saw the girl charge out the door. She turned to Mya, "Humph, she didn't even say good-bye." Then Mrs. Chinkley brushed her hands back and forth, smacking them as if she'd just cleaned up and said, "Well, that takes care of her!"

Mya quickly came over to the counter to where Mrs. Chinkley had started wiping off the pears that had just come in. She said, "Mrs. Chinkley, I didn't know that you knew my teacher, Mrs. Braxton." Her eyes widened with the look of surprise on her face.

With the fingers of her left hand scratching her forehead, Mrs. Chinkley said, "I just want to make sure of something. Franka Martin was one of the girls who was pelting you with snowballs, wasn't she?"

Mya hadn't known how clever Mrs. Chinkley was until now. "Yes, she was," Mya admitted, "but how did you know?"

Mrs. Chinkley winked an eye and said, "Honey, I was a kid once and, remember, I had my share of run-ins with bullies, too. I thought I would try helping you out a little. I could tell by the look on your face that she was someone you didn't want here. And by her attitude, I knew that she was up to no good. Seeing her reaction, I think I was right."

"Did you call Mrs. Braxton on the phone?" asked Mya. "You know it wasn't true what she said about me. I always get my homework done. Franka lied."

"I thought as much," said Mrs. Chinkley. "But, to be honest, that wasn't your teacher on the phone. I don't even know the woman. I was just pretending to make a call to her. Pretty convincing, wasn't I? I should have been an actress." She smiled to herself. Then she turned her face to Mya and said, "You know, bullies aren't as smart as they think they are. And sometimes, you have to play their silly games to outwit them."

A lot of laughter could be heard coming from the market that afternoon. And one thing was for sure. Mya had her job for as long as she wanted, and now she knew the meaning of true friendship.

Discussion Questions

 Mrs. Chinkley was a quick thinker. She saw Mya's reaction to Franka Martin's visit to the market so she threw a coughing fit. Why was this a great way to distract Franka and stop Mya from interfering?

 Why did Mrs. Chinkley want to handle Franka all by herself and not let Mya deal with the bully?

 Mrs. Chinkley pretended to know Laura Braxton, the girls' teacher. Lying is a bad thing. Do you feel it was right for Mrs. Chinkley to pretend she knew the teacher? Explain your reasons.

Good Riddance

If Mya could, she would have erased the memory of Franka Martin asking for her job. She would love to forget the lie about her homework, which was mean and vicious. If she had the opportunity to let these thoughts go, she would jump at the chance.

Is there a memory you would like to be rid of? Have you experienced something that bothers you every time the thought comes in your head?

On the next page, you will see a drawing of a person's head. Imagine it is your head filled with memories, thoughts, and images, like a TV screen. These memories of your life float around your head and, whenever something reminds you, you call up the thought like tuning into a TV show.

There are happy memories and some unfortunate ones. If you could erase those most embarrassing moments, your unhappiest times, or the things you are most ashamed of, you would be free of self-criticism and self-doubt.

In a large thought bubble above the head, draw a memory of an unfortunate moment in your life. Use a pencil. Wait until everyone in the class has done the same. Be ready to say good-bye to this memory.

The next step is to have a *Good Riddance Ceremony.* Your teacher can light a candle or flashlight, say a few final words about these hurtful memories, and ask students to ready their erasers. At the count of three, everyone in the class must erase the bad memories from their bubbles. As students erase the memories at the same time, they will feel a release hearing the sound of erasers rubbing away the unfortunate moments from their memories. Once these thoughts are gone, they will lose their power. Good riddance!

ACTIVITY 1, STORY #8: MRS. CHINKLEY HAS SOMETHING UP HER SLEEVE (continued)

The Bully-Proof Vest

ACTIVITY 2, STORY #8: MRS. CHINKLEY HAS SOMETHING UP HER SLEEVE

Bullies love when those who are bullied show how upset they are. Mya may have shown her worried face to Franka if Mrs. Chinkley hadn't stopped her. Bullies love having a reason to come back and bully again. Seeing pain in someone's expression gives bullies such enjoyment, they crave to see it over and over.

Wouldn't it be nice to have some kind of protection? Policemen, presidents, and pilots wear bulletproof vests to protect themselves from being shot by criminals. These vests are made of a special material that deflects bullets. Wouldn't you like wearing something like that when a bully calls you names, says words that belittle you, or tries to tease you to make you feel bad?

One way to protect yourself is to catch the bully off guard. Look for something humorous in the situation. Find something funny to laugh at, so that the attack is not so serious. A joke may stop a bully from going on. Humor often breaks up a serious moment and changes anger into laughter. If a bully is belittling you, knowing a few jokes might make you laugh. The bully may even enjoy a little joke, too. Jokes will definitely help you feel better after the attack when you can't find anything funny about the bullying.

If Mya knew a joke about snow, perhaps she wouldn't have felt so bad about the ambush. Jokes and humor can be your bully-proof vest.

Here is a bully joke: *What do you get when you cross a bully with a lizard? ...A blizzard!*

Your task is:
- Find some jokes you love and write them on the lines around the vest below.
- Memorize them and the next time you feel worried or nervous, tell yourself a joke. Laughing makes you feel better. Try one on your "favorite bully." Who knows, the bully may see you as a funny person instead of a weak one.

Both Sides of the Story

ACTIVITY 3, STORY #8: MRS. CHINKLEY HAS SOMETHING UP HER SLEEVE

Let's look into the mind of someone who tries to make you feel unsure of yourself. There are probably lots of reasons why bullies abuse people. Perhaps they are unsure of themselves. They may be trying to cover up their own weaknesses.

There are pros and cons to bullying. Pros are things bullies like about bullying. Cons are the things people hate about being bullied.

Once you look at both sides of the story, you may be able to understand what drives someone to put others down. If Mya could understand what Franka and Bonnita were thinking when they picked on her, she might have been able to avoid them. If she thought like a bully, she would see situations the way bullies see them. She would see the joy they got out of chasing her. She could feel the control they had over her.

Once you see what makes someone take advantage of another person, you will be able to dodge a bully. You will be one step ahead of them. Once they know they cannot take advantage of you, you will not be bullied ever again.

This is your task:
Fill in the chart on the next page, writing in the pros and cons of bullying. The first one has been done for you. You will soon see what bullies get out of bullying.

Bullying Chart

PROS Why do bullies love to bully?	CONS Why do kids hate to be bullied?
Bullies feel powerful when they make someone cry.	Crying makes a person feel weak and babyish.

Stop Bullying Forever

In the previous activity you filled in a chart showing the pros and cons of bullying. You were able to see the bully-side and non-bully side of the argument. Now it is time to turn this information into a piece of persuasive writing, arguing why bullying is a despicable act.

Your job is to convince the bullies of the world to stop bullying. Make their arguments look weak. Describe the fear people feel every time they come near bullies who try to hurt them. If you write a strong enough argument against bullying, bullies may actually see how wrong they are and change their behavior forever.

Here is an example to help you get started. There is also a persuasive essay on the next page to see what it is like. It is not quite the same topic, but it may help you when it comes time to plan your essay.

Should Mya Tell Mrs. Braxton About the Bullies?

PROS	CONS
Mrs. Braxton will be aware of their cruel behaviors.	Mya will look like a tattletale.
Mrs. Braxton can speak to the bullies to get them to stop.	Mya looks weak and powerless.
Mya is able to share her problem with someone.	Mrs. Braxton has seen no proof that Mya is being bullied.

Persuasive Essay: Mya Must Tell Mrs. Braxton

Mya McGreggor is totally alone in her classroom. She has no one to protect her from Franka Martin and Bonnita Campbell. That must be a terrible feeling. She needs a friend to help her stand up against the bullies. The most powerful person to come to her aid is Mrs. Braxton, her teacher. This woman needs to be aware of the cruel behaviors these girls have shown Mya. Unfortunately, she never sees when it happens.

When Bonnita and Franka were mean to Mya on the playground, calling her names and behaving badly, Mya should have gone to her teacher. After all, she was a new girl in the classroom and Mrs. Braxton would have understood how scared she was. She wouldn't have thought Mya was a tattletale. She would have seen how badly they hurt Mya by noticing her tears.

If she talks to her teacher about the bullying, Mrs. Braxton can speak to the girls and make them stop their attacks. It is not a sign of weakness to ask for help. She can get their parents involved too.

Sometimes adults have good ideas because they may have had the same experience. For example, look at what Mrs. Chinkley did when she pretended to call Mrs. Braxton. She knew what to do and it made Mya feel stronger. Because she and her family were once bullied, she didn't see Mya as a weakling at all. She saw the proof with her own eyes as she picked Mya off the sidewalk. Bullying does a lot of damage.

Perhaps speaking to the teacher would teach the bullies a very needed lesson. They must learn that they can not get away with bullying. It is time we all stand up to bullies to end bullying forever.

■ This persuasive essay gives both sides of the story to make the point clear. Remember your essay will be about *Ways to Stop Bullying*.

■ Once you've written your essay on your own paper, plan for a whole class reading of these arguments against bullying. Invite the neighbors in. Use the *Grading Rubric For Speeches*, Activity 4, pages 87 and 88, to score the presentations.

Unit 9:

THE
RESCUE

Finally Some Kindness

Mya befriends Meowy, the landlord's cat, when she rescues it from a dangerous situation. Somehow, the cat gets a fishhook stuck in its lip and, with Momma's help, mother and daughter save the cat. A bond between Mya and her mother begins to develop.

Lesson	Objectives	Student Goals	Materials and Lesson	Insights	Author's Message
Story #9 **Finally Some Kindness**	Students gain new knowledge about Mya and Momma in this latest story. The landlord's ignored and unwanted cat needs help and Mya discovers a new connection with Momma over the cat's predicament.	The cat draws mother and daughter together when no other experience has united this relationship. Readers see a new, gentler Momma, as does Mya. Students conclude that the cat seems to have some sort of special power.	Students need a copy of the text. It can be read aloud to students, or they can read it silently. Small groups can also read together.	Meowy's life parallels Mya's. She is disrespected and feels unwanted like Mya. Perhaps this is why they seem to find comfort in each other's company.	Momma has a lo animals and a so place in her heart wounded ones. Mother and daug find that they bot have a common The cat seems to the power to draw them together in unexpected and satisfying way.
Discussion Questions	These questions encourage students to explain why Meowy once came to Mya's window for help, why Momma was not angry with Mya for taking the cat in, and why there was jealousy in Mya's heart as she watched Momma relate to the cat.	Students see the change that comes over Momma after dealing with the wounded cat. Momma seems gentler and kinder to her daughter. Why is she so kind to the cat while treating its problem? Would the cat be the link that joins Momma and Mya together?	Students need the discussion questions and a copy of the text to look for the answers. There is an opportunity for open dialogue among students in the form of large group conversations.	Momma must have seen something in Mya's eyes. Perhaps it was the same look she saw in Meowy's eyes. It was the look of hurt, abandonment, and disregard. That look plucked a string in her heart.	This chapter show change in the relationship betwe Mya and Momma sees a different sic Momma and Mon perceives sadness little girl. She sees same sadness in t eyes of an abused disrespected
Activity 1: **Make Someone Feel Good**	Students help others by showing kindness to their peers. They practice good deeds that are listed on the worksheet.	Students keep track of their attempts at being kind to others, especially those who display signs of being left out or unsure of themselves. One side effect is that students experience a change in their own attitudes towards others and themselves.	Students need a pencil, a copy of the worksheet, and time to plan ways to accomplish good deeds. They record their activities over a period of time and look for results. Their goal will be to keep a record, explain how the kindnesses were done, and look for proof that they were successful.	Mya and Meowy were drawn together by a common bond. This bond was very obvious to Momma. As she extended kindness to the cat, Momma saw a bond growing between the animal and her daughter. From then on she looked at her daughter through different eyes.	We must be compassionate to our fellow beings because we are a connected. This compassion return us in positive wa Momma and My extended compa to a wounded an and in return discovered a ne loving relationsh
Activity 2: **You've Done a Nice Thing**	Students send messages of kindness on a form titled You've Done a Nice Thing. They become watchdogs as they observe their class-mates doing good deeds. They secretly fill out and deliver these notices to the people who display kind behaviors in the classroom.	Students realize that when someone receives a kind message, it is uplifting. These handwritten notes reinforce a person's good traits. They can be collected and reread.	Students need the worksheet and a pencil. They also need several copies of the form. Extra forms can be placed in a special place in the room where students can easily obtain them. As students observe kindnesses, they fill out and deliver these forms.	The funny thing about kindness is that when we perform a kind act for someone else, it lifts our own spirits.	Students look for ness in the world around them, start the classroom. Too world is filled with ness, fear, and uncertainty. Scho filled with stress a worry. Looking for goodness, kindne compassion in ou environment brin joy and encourag spirits to soar.
Activity 3: **Solve the Mystery Words**	Students play a word game to solve story mysteries. The words have common sounds but different spellings and meanings. All mysteries relate to Mya's experiences. As students solve the clues, they also think about Mya's life.	Students delve into the experiences Mya has had throughout the story. As students work out the answers, they practice their story knowledge, phonemic understanding, and spelling skills.	Students need the worksheet, a pencil, and a partner. Students read the questions and write answers based on clues from the story.	There is a connection between this activity and the theme of the unit.	Students notice a common bond a the words that an the questions. Eac has the "ear" sou Not surprisingly, theme of this uni also bonding or connections.
Activity 4: **Friendship Notes**	Students attempt to change peoples' lives by writing unexpected Friendship Notes.	The message on these notes simply offers friendship. Students anonymously send friendly messages to those in need, in and outside the classroom.	Students need the work-sheet, a pencil, and paper to write notes. They look for those in need of a friend and compose a simple note. They deliver the note and observe the response.	It feels good to send encouraging messages.	We all need to he something good, not just on specia casions. Students to enjoy the simp of freely offering a kind words when are unexpected.

FINALLY SOME KINDNESS

Mya's homework was done and she had just tucked herself in bed. It was about nine o'clock on a Thursday evening and she was almost ready to drift off to sleep. Outside her window the night looked frozen. Mya lay in her bed almost asleep when she heard a noise. Her thoughts took her to the living room where Momma had the television on. She could hear TV voices through her bedroom door but she knew the sound was not a television sound.

She heard it again. The noise was like a cry for help. She sat up in bed. It sounded like a whimpering animal. Mya got up and tiptoed over to her window. Her room was on the first floor and she looked out, but it was very dark. The streetlight barely lit up the side yard. Mya's window overlooked the road and all she could see was a blue darkness covering the whole snowy yard. It looked empty. Mya took another scan before she let out a sigh of relief and crept back into bed, thinking it was probably her imagination.

No sooner had she pulled up the covers when there came another cry. This time it was a little louder and seemed closer. She got up to take another look. She was able to look down into the crunchy, dried-up leaves that had gathered below her window to escape the winds.

She decided to stick her head outside and have a closer look. She knew Momma would not approve of what she was doing so she quietly raised the window and pushed her head out. It was icy cold and her breath made clouds with each exhale. She scanned the area right next to the wall of the house. She felt shivers under her thin pajamas. Something moved and it caught her eye. She automatically turned toward the direction of a tiny whimper coming from the pile of frosty leaves.

She spotted an animal lying very still. To her amazement, it was Meowy, the landlord's cat. She seemed to be in some sort of anguish because she had a very serious look on her face. She blinked her usual blink to Mya and turned up her chin.

As she called to Meowy, Mya didn't notice anything strange about the cat. There was no blood, no scratches, and no bruises. She knew the cat didn't look as if she had been wounded but Mya decided to investigate further. She hung herself out the window and gently wrapped her warm hands around the cat's middle. Mya knew something was wrong because the cat let Mya take her up in her arms and bring her into the bedroom. This was unusual for the skittish cat. She shut the window and began to talk to the cat.

"Meowy," she whispered, "What is going on with you tonight? You don't look very hurt, but you sound like you are."

She sat Meowy down on the bed and began inspecting her all over. She lifted the cat's grayish legs, looked in her ears, and even checked her underbelly. At first, she didn't see anything wrong. She almost let the cat go but decided to take one more careful look. That's when she saw it.

There was something hanging from Meowy's lip. It was the same gray color as the cat but definitely was not supposed to be there. She furrowed her eyebrows and squinted to see what hung there. Mya's eyebrows lifted when she realized what it was. There was a fishhook stuck through Meowy's lip, but there was no blood and no fishing line, just a hook. Her mind zoomed as it tried to imagine how in the world Meowy got a fishhook stuck in her lip, in January. And where did she find that fishhook, anyway?

She remembered a conversation she recently had with Bobby Blanko, the landlord's son. He had told her that there was a nice pond in the woods behind her house. Bobby had been outside shoveling the sidewalk and mentioned the pond and how he loved going skating there in winter and fishing in the summer. They were talking about what they each liked to do best. He seemed a lot nicer than his father, Mr. Blanko. Mya liked talking to Bobby.

As she looked at the cat, she said aloud, "It does look like a brand new hook, thank goodness. That means no infection." Then she added, "Meowy, what have you been up to? Don't you know it is winter? Maybe you have been planning on doing some ice fishing down at the pond." Mya laughed out loud.

The cat didn't seem to find that very funny. She just blinked and raised her chin as if to say, "Do something, please!"

"Mya, I thought I heard you talking to someone," Momma said as she barged into the room without knocking. "I came in to say good n.... What is that you have there on your bed?" Mya was worried at seeing Momma come in and tried to cover Meowy with the quilt but it was too late. Momma, of course, had already seen the cat. "Well, what have we here?" Momma asked.

Mya was very surprised at the kind look on Momma's face. Usually she was upset about the things she caught Mya doing, especially when it was something she didn't like. Mya nervously explained the whimpering sound she had heard when she was trying to fall asleep. She explained how she found Meowy outside her window looking so sad. She showed Momma the fishhook in Meowy's lip. She told Momma who owned the cat.

Suddenly, Momma said something that shocked her daughter. She didn't act angry or annoyed at Mya for bringing the cat into her bedroom. Momma simply said, "Well, if we want this beautiful cat to live a long healthy life, we'd better take care of her right now. I'm sure she will appreciate our kindness."

Momma inspected the lip and took pity on the cat. "Oh, you poor baby," she said. "I think we can fix you up." Her gentle hand stroked the whole length of the cat as she looked up at Mya. Momma saw a look in her daughter's eyes that melted her heart. Then she looked at the wounded animal. She smiled and told Mya to hang on to the cat while she ran to get something from the kitchen. Mya had no idea what Momma was up to, but she waited, holding Meowy on her lap and petted the cat gently.

By now Meowy had stretched herself out across the girl's lap seeming to know that help was on the way. Meowy's two front legs stretched out over one side of Mya's lap like superman flying through the atmosphere. Her back legs and tail draped over Mya's other leg, blending into the bed coverings.

It was strange but Mya felt herself calming down too, just petting Meowy and knowing that Momma was coming to the rescue. The cat purred and Mya felt her own breath slowing down. At first she worried thinking about how they could help the cat at this late hour but with Momma taking over, everything seemed as though it would be fine.

Meowy was helping Mya stay calm while Momma had a plan to help the troubled cat. Soon Momma was back with some wire cutters and a tube of anti-germ cream.

She said, "Mya, you hold onto the cat and keep petting her. Try to keep her head still. Comfort her with assuring words. I am going to cut the outside part of the hook and when it falls apart, it will come out of her lip and she will be just fine. It doesn't look rusty. I have some anti-germ cream just in case. Tomorrow you can tell Mr. Blanko or Bobby so one of them can take her to the vet. How in the world did she get this hook in her lip?"

Mya again was shocked. Momma was being so sweet to the cat. She found herself feeling a little jealous but she did as she was told and soon Meowy was hookless. Momma snipped the hook apart without a problem. It dropped off into her hand just as Momma had said it would. Mya secretly wished Momma was this gentle with her when she was in trouble. The anti-germ cream was gently rubbed on the cat's lip. Momma put the cap on the tube and Mya continued to pet the cat.

"Now Mya, it is time for bed. You have school tomorrow and I have work." said Momma. " I think you had better release her just the way she came in." Mya carried Meowy over to the window and opened it. She leaned over to gently place the cat where she was found. As if to say thank you, Meowy blinked at her two nurses and ran off into the darkness. Momma hugged Mya tenderly and kissed her gently on the forehead. "You'll make a great nurse one day," she whispered. As the door closed,

Mya thanked Momma for helping Meowy. Momma poked her head back into the room and said, "That was a nice thing you did, rescuing the cat." Then she blew her daughter a kiss and left.

She felt a new closeness to her mother that night and saw that they finally had something in common: a soft place in their hearts for helpless animals. Mya never knew this about Momma. In her wildest dreams she never thought kindness would somehow bring them together. Her heart was full and she closed her eyes with a warm feeling in her chest.

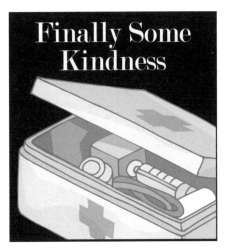

Discussion Questions

 Why do you think Meowy asked for Mya's help rather than the Blankos'?

 Why didn't Momma react with anger and punishment when she found Mya with the wounded cat?

 Mya began to feel jealous as she watched Momma tend to the cat. Why was there such jealousy in her heart?

Make Someone Feel Good

ACTIVITY 1, STORY #9: FINALLY SOME KINDNESS

Lots of people have low self-esteem. Bullies, in fact, act like they are confident. However, deep inside they actually feel inadequate and dislike themselves. Think of Bonnita and Franka. In Chapter 6, when Franka was absent from school, Bonnita acted normal. When they got together, they became evil. Perhaps if they were recognized for the nice things they did, they would stop bullying.

Meowy felt bullied because of the way Mr. Blanko treated her. She was ignored and kicked. She didn't go to him when she was in trouble. She went to someone she thought would show her kindness. She sensed that Mya also felt unloved. Perhaps that is why she went to Mya for help rather then her owners. Somehow Meowy knew that she and Mya shared the same fate. They must have felt the connection when their eyes met.

In this activity, you will spread kindness to others. A chart on the next page is filled with ideas you can use to make others feel better. There are suggestions for showing small kindnesses to others. You can record your activities and observations as you perform these tasks.

Once you accomplish each task, write what process you used. Watch for proof that shows the person felt better as a direct result of your kindness. Doing something nice for Meowy brought Momma and Mya closer together. Helping others warms our hearts. It can work for bullies too. You may also notice a change in yourself as you see how good you make others feel.

Feel Good Idea	How Did You Accomplish This?	What Proof Shows You Were Successful?	Date Done
Call someone you wouldn't normally call at night for a short chat about homework.			
Pick someone who's always left out to be on your team.			
Invite a shy student over to play.			
Sit next to someone you don't normally hang out with.			
Get next to a different person in line.			
Save a spot for a new friend the next time you sit in a group.			
Ask to be on a different team than you are usually on.			
Encourage those who don't feel confident.			
Ask to be a reading or math helper.			
Plan doing homework with a new friend.			
Mention the things you respect about your friends.			
Work on a project with someone who needs your help.			
Say nice things about others whenever you are with them.			
Defend strangers if others misjudge them.			
Stop someone from saying bad things behind others' backs.			
Extend kindness to animals in need.			
Show your appreciation when you are helped.			

You've Done a Nice Thing

ACTIVITY 2, STORY #9: FINALLY SOME KINDNESS

Your task for this activity will be to watch the goings on in your classroom. Look for students being kind and offering help to those in need. As you saw Mya save Meowy from the fishhook, you will be watching for students doing nice things.

On the next page, notice the form entitled: **YOU'VE DONE A NICE THING**. This document is a reward for doing good deeds. Once you see a good deed being done, fill out a form and deliver it to the classmate who did it. Whenever you catch someone doing a nice thing for someone else, without being asked, fill out another form. Extra copies of the form should be stored in a place where you can easily find them.

As you thoughtfully write what you noticed, use words that make the receiver feel good about the nice thing that was done. Have fun making others feel great. It is up to you if you want to sign it. Hopefully, you will receive some yourself. Make a collection and store them in a journal or scrapbook. Reread them when you feel blue or depressed. They will cheer your heart.

YOU'VE DONE A NICE THING

DATE: _____

This Document Certifies That

_____

Was Observed Performing a Kind Deed.

HERE IS WHAT I SAW:

_____

_____

_____

_____

YOUR FRIEND,

_____

Save this document and make a collection to remind you of how special you are and how wonderful it was to think of someone else.

ACTIVITY 3, STORY #9: FINALLY SOME KINDNESS

This activity is about drawing conclusions based on evidence. Mya knew that the cat had been whimpering and lifting its head. Based on that, she looked for signs of trouble. You, too, can be a detective and try to solve some word mysteries.

All the mystery words on the next page have something in common. They all have the same sound in them. The sound *"ear"* is in each mystery word but it is spelled several ways: *ear, eer,* or *ere*. Your goal, besides guessing the word, is to spell each word correctly.

All the words or phrases relate to Mya's life experiences from the story. Use the word bank to help you draw conclusions about your selections, based on the evidence in each sentence.

Salty liquids or _____ fell from Mya's eyes when Franka and Bonnita pelted her with snowballs.

_____ , an emotion that ran through Mya's mind when she heard Mrs. Braxton call her to read, caused her to freeze up.

When someone sings a mean-spirited chant like Bonnita and Franka, the chant is called a _____ .

Mya's classmates are called her _____ .

At Chinkley's Produce Market, Mya stacked oranges that were shaped like_____ .

Meowy was very_____ the side of the house, crouching in the leaves."

Mrs. Chinkley spoke_____ as she told Mya about her own past dealings with a bully named Mr. Calhoon.

Bonnita and Franka were crystal _____ about how they disliked Mya.

Mya wished her problems with bullies would_____ .

Mya_____ and never gave up no matter how badly she was treated by Franka and Bonnita.

WORD BANK

clear	peers	jeer	persevered	fear
tears	sincerely	disappear	spheres	near

Friendship Notes

ACTIVITY 4, STORY #9: FINALLY SOME KINDNESS

Kind words can change a person's life for the better. Handwritten messages of kindness are touching and revealing. In this activity you will be writing and sending *Friendship Notes*. Mya could have used a friendship note to cheer her. Kindness was not in her classmates' thoughts. Luckily, Mya practiced kindness herself when she took Meowy under her wing and saved the cat when there was a need.

Look around you. Find a person who seems to be in need of a friend. It can be in your own classroom, on your bus, in your neighborhood, or someone who is sick in a hospital or nursing home. In fact, everybody needs a friend because friends listen, care for, and support their pals when they can.

A friendly, hand-written message is one of the best ways to help someone feel better when things are going bad. Writing a personal note can change moods. It can lift spirits. Writing sticks in our minds because it can be reread whenever needed. We don't send enough friendship notes. We usually send cards or letters but only when there is a holiday or birthday. Why not send notes when there is no special reason?

Notes can be anonymous and secretly passed. They are perfect ways to make someone feel special. They are better than gifts.

In this activity, your task will be to:

■ Find a person who is in need of a *Friendship Note*.

■ Write one in your best writing that says nice things and makes cheerful statements. You may or may not wish to sign it.

■ Secretly deliver the note and place it somewhere so it is sure to be found.

■ Watch for joyous expressions as the note is opened and read.

■ Enjoy sending a message to someone. Be proud and give away the gift of friendship freely.

SOMEONE NEW TO BULLY

STORY #10 SUMMARY

New Boy

Steven Frangelli joins Mya's class. He doesn't seem very strong so Mya takes him under her wing. She predicts that the bullies will go after him and they do. She boldly plans to defend him against the bullies, no matter what.

son	Objectives	Student Goals	Materials and Lesson	Insights	Author's Message
#10	Mya buddies up with the new student, Steven Frangelli. She feels good about herself as she helps him fit into the classroom routines.	Students find that one good deed leads to another. Steven and Mya do have a great deal in common. Mya quickly takes him under her wing and bonds with him because she knows what it is like to be new and friendless.	Students need a copy of the text. It can be read aloud to students, or they can read it silently. Small groups can also read together.	Mya did not take pity on Steven. She did not volunteer to help him just because no one else did. She recognized all the signs of feeling different, separate, and unwelcome. He reminded Mya of herself.	Students must understand that being new to a classroom is difficult. Everyone knows each other, friends have already grouped together, and proving yourself is very challenging and sometimes dis-appointing. She had been through it herself.
ussion stions	These questions encourage students to explain why Mya made some interesting observations about Steven, why she felt she made a good decision to buddy up with him, and why his friendship gave her more confidence.	Students gain insight into how Mya thinks. She seemed to feel bolder having Steven in the classroom and re-alized that he would become a good friend to her. He showed her kindness by helping her think through a math problem. This was something she had not experienced in that classroom thus far.	Students need the discussion questions and a copy of the text to look for the answers. There is an opportunity for open dialogue among students in the form of large group conversations.	When dealing with bullies, two is better than one and two against two is even better.	Volunteering is an opportunity to help someone in need and, in return, you yourself are helped. Mya discovered this very quickly as she and Steven became good friends.
vity 1: a n z	Students analyze how they solve math story problems by answering a series of questions. They think about how they process information to achieve an answer.	Students gain insight as they realize that they actually have many skills when it comes to understanding and solving problems. They develop confidence in their ability.	Students need a pencil, a copy of the worksheet, and time to answer the questions. The questions all relate to their mathematical knowledge.	Students learn to appreciate their personal skills in mathematical thinking. They gain insight into the way they reason.	Mathematical reasoning is a very important skill. It is logical, analytical thinking that also helps one solve life's problems.
vity 2: erstanding hematics	Students gather information from the previous activity, You are a Math Whiz, and compose a paragraph that restates what they do as mathematical thinkers.	Students see their own problem solving skills all written out. They realize that they have more abilities than they thought.	Students need the worksheet, a pencil, and time to work on the composition. Using the answers they wrote in the previous activity, they piece together an essay that clearly identifies and explains how they solve math story problems.	It is important to take pride in accomplish-ments, no matter how small or insignificant we think they are. It is necessary to take an accounting of our successes rather than always tracking our failures.	Mya knew that her math skills were foggy and felt rather embarrassed to ask questions of the teacher. She did not wish to be ridiculed by the bullies for her lack of knowledge. She was certain they would notice if she asked a silly question. Luckily, Steven made her feel comfortable enough to ask a question which he treated with respect rather than criticism.
vity 3: mittees New ents	The class develops a plan to acclimate new students to the classroom when they arrive.	Students brainstorm activities for each committee. Committees then select practices that will make the classroom seem more inviting to new arrivals.	Students need the worksheet and a pencil. As a class, they list ideas under each committee to help new students acclimate. Each committee contributes a project to welcome new students to the room.	All too often curriculum takes precedence over hospitality. New students are usually assigned a buddy. This doesn't necessarily make them feel like part of the group.	New arrivals often look and feel lost when they come into a new situation. Helping them feel a part of what goes on by filling in the gaps can link the whole class together as a community.
vity 4: a mittee	Students look over the ideas listed for each committee and select one they wish to join.	Students participate in the planning and completion of artifacts their committee creates to welcome new students.	Students need the worksheet, a pencil, and time to meet with committees to develop pamphlets, charts, histories, and advice columns to acclimate new students.	Each classroom needs to make newcomers feel at ease.	A sense of belonging is very important to every individual. Feeling like an outsider gives a student reason to act out or perhaps bully.

NEW BOY

It was a few weeks later when Mya's classroom underwent a big change. Mya was trying to get a math assignment done so she wouldn't have any homework. As she was working hard that morning, there came a knock at the classroom door. Mrs. Braxton barely opened it when the principal, Mrs. Dewey, and a new boy, rushed in.

Steven Frangelli was introduced to the class. The principal rushed out mumbling something about a meeting she had to go to. Steven was left there looking down at his shoes. His curly blond hair draped over his eyes, as he stood very still right next to Mrs. Braxton. His pants were baggy. His shirt looked like it could fit a football linebacker as it came to the top of his knees. He seemed so small standing by the door. Mya decided he unfortunately was just the right size to be picked on. In fact, the way he hunched his shoulders over, it looked like he already had some experience at being bullied and pushed around.

He hardly said hello to Mrs. Braxton. She shook his hand and his whole arm wobbled around like a wet noodle. It was as if he wasn't sure how to shake hands. Probably he was afraid. It is hard to be the new kid, Mya thought. She knew what that was like.

Mrs. Braxton showed him the desk. It was next to Mya's and she already had a plan to save him from the class bullies. She was raring to go.

He never looked up as he walked over to his new desk. She remembered being new and how it felt not to see a friendly face anywhere. In this classroom everybody knew each other. They sent the message that they did not want to know Steven. He picked the safest place to look, down. She glanced over at Bonnita and Franka, the "ringleaders of hate." They were already making faces, rolling their eyes, and whispering to each other. Mya could just about guess what they were saying. It was then she decided she had a friend in the class after all.

Mrs. Braxton told the class to welcome Steven Frangelli. Most of the class said, "Hi," without looking up. When Mrs. Braxton asked for a volunteer to buddy up with Steven, Mya quickly raised her hand and was selected. She noticed there was no other hand up. The girl who was her buddy had moved away the day after Mya arrived. Mya was left "buddy-less," until now.

She thought she would try to protect Steven from the things she went through so she walked right over to his desk to welcome him personally. He hardly looked up at her and seemed to be lost in thought. She grabbed all the books he needed and helped to place them in his desk. She found the math page they were working on and donated her own paper. She offered him a brand new flag-covered pencil. Steven perked up when he saw the pencil. He finally looked up at Mya and she smiled at him. "My name's Mya," she said.

"Go ahead, it's yours," she offered. "I hope that pencil brings you good luck on doing that page," she pointed to the math work. "I am pretty new in this class, too. Don't worry, I'll help you fit in." She whispered in his right ear, "I am glad you are here." She gave him an assuring smile and went back to her math work.

Steven started on the page and was finished before Mya got to the fifth problem. She'd been working on number four long before he came into the room. He looked over at Mya and gave her a tiny smile. He whispered, "Math is my best subject. Let me know if you need help."

Mya realized she had made a perfect choice when she volunteered to be Steven's buddy. Not only had she done something nice for him but she had also done something nice for herself. Math was hard for her.

"Number five," she whispered. "I think you add but I am not sure. Am I right?"

Steven looked over the problem and he read the words "in all," underlining them with his finger. He held up his book, pointed to those words, and whispered, "'In all' is like when you put your crayons away. When you count them to see that you have them all, you are adding. So, yes, you are right! Good job." Somehow Steven knew in his mind that he could help Mya, too. So what if she was a girl.

Mya smiled to herself. Steven had made the math question so simple to understand that she knew he would be of great help to her. Then she turned her eyes toward Franka and raised her eyebrows with a tiny spurt of movement. Just as she fixed her gaze on the girl, Franka glared back and cupped her hand around her mouth. She whispered to Bonnita and they began to laugh. Mya could just imagine their jokes about Steven and Mya but she didn't care. Now she had an ally. Two is better that one, especially when going up against bullies.

New Boy

Discussion Questions

 Mya made an observation about Steven Frangelli. She thought his hunched-over shoulders made him look like he had already experienced being bullied. What did she mean by that?

 Mya realized she had made a perfect choice when she volunteered to be Steven's buddy. What convinced her that this was true?

 As Mya thought about her new friend Steven, she realized how he might be a great help to her. In fact, she felt a certain sense of power in her bold move as she turned her eyes toward Franka, raised her eyebrows, and stared at the girl. What was going through Mya's mind?

You Are a Math Whiz

ACTIVITY 1, STORY #10: NEW BOY

How do you solve math story problems? Steven had no trouble with them but Mya was very unsure of herself. You may be surprised to find that you have a lot of tools to help you. You may use the pictures to clue you in on what the question is asking. You probably look at the words very carefully and reread them if you are puzzled. You may realize that the wording in a problem reminds you of phrases you have seen before.

The questions below will point out that you really know more than you think. As you answer these questions, be proud of yourself. Realize that you have many tools to solve math problems using your own good thinking skills. It is better to rely on your own abilities, then to constantly ask for help. Math skills improve much faster when you depend on your own knowledge.

Here are the questions. Please fill in the answers.

■ When you look at a question, how do you decide what the story problem is asking you to do?

_____

■ Tell how you use your memory to help you solve the math problem. Give an example.

_____

_____

■ What word clues in a question tell you whether to add, subtract, multiply, or divide?

_____

■ If a problem has several steps, how do you know what to do to get the final answer?

_____

■ Drawing pictures helps. Tell about how you use drawings to decide on math processes.

_____

■ Was there a time when you had to draw to solve a hard problem? _____
How did visualizing make the question clear?

_____

■ What do you do when you come to a problem that completely confuses you?

_____

■ How are you able to decide what to do when you are on your own?

_____

■ Why is it better to look for help in the book rather than ask the teacher?

_____

■ What is the best thing to do when you get stuck on a word problem?

■ Where else can you get help?

■ When is it best to ask someone for help?

■ If you are reading a story problem and the words do not make sense to you, what do you do?

■ What do you do to understand the words in a story problem?

■ Describe how it feels to work a few math problems correctly.

■ What does "smart" feel like?

■ How do you know when you understand the story problem?

■ Do you ever try to help others who are confused?

■ How does it feel to help others, as Steven did?

■ What is the most fun about math?

■ Tell how you use notes, past assignments, or the textbook to help you solve math problems.

■ How was Mya's way of questioning better than asking for the answer?

■ How have you helped your neighbor think through a problem?

■ What happens when you constantly ask for the teacher's help?

■ How do you feel on math test day?

In this activity, you will put your answers together and write a paragraph about all the things you do as a Math Whiz. You may be happily surprised when you are finished. You probably know more than you thought. When you see it all written out, you'll enjoy the confidence that comes over you. Math is something you will use the rest of your life.

Write your paragraph here. Use the information from Activity 1.

I Consider Myself a Math Whiz

Committees For New Students

When new students enter your classroom, how are they greeted? In Steven's case, he was rushed into the room, the principal left for a meeting, and the teacher just announced his name to the class. Then she took him to his new desk. Luckily there was a buddy system and Mya volunteered to help him. Imagine how he felt coming into this unfriendly room. He didn't want to be there anymore than the class wanted him.

In this activity, you will develop a plan for new students who enter your room. As a class, brainstorm project plans for the committees on the chart below. Each committee will plan and design a section of the *New Student Information Kit*. Committees may choose to make a booklet, pamphlet, folder, chart, newsletter, diary, timeline, log, or any other artifact. Whatever they create, it must be included in the kit to be given to new arrivals.

Fill in the Chart with suggestions and ideas. Each committee then picks the one project they wish to work on.

COMMITTEE PROJECT CHART

Student Information	Class History	Rules and Regulations	Homework Information	Volunteer Buddies	Supplies And Work Samples	Adv
Example: Class Pictures	Biographies					

Join a Committee

In this activity you will join one of the committees. Look at the chart below and circle the name of committee that appeals to your creativity. Then list six things that you will personally contribute to this committee's activities. You may wish to head up the committee or simply work on a particular part of the final project. Meet with your committee and tell what you will do to add to the completed project.

When all committee work is done, projects will be combined to form your classroom's *New Student Information Kit*. As a new student enters your room, the kit will be explained by one of the committees so that the new arrival will be made to feel part of the group. Ask the student to take it home and look at it as a homework assignment. This kit makes for good community relations. Each student who enters your room will enjoy leafing through the kit, looking it over and discussing it with family. A strong sense of belonging will emerge. There is no better feeling than being accepted, especially when you are new in town.

COMMITTEE PROJECT CHART

Student Information	Class History	Rules and Regulations	Homework Information	Volunteer Buddies	Supplies And Work Samples	Advisors

Unit 11:

SECOND PLAYGROUND ATTACK

Steven Gets Even

The bullies attack Steven on the playground when Mya is not around. The attack is very similar to Mya's. When she arrives on the playground to find Steven under siege, she comes to his rescue.

son	Objectives	Student Goals	Materials and Lesson	Insights	Author's Message
#11 en n	Students read about the second bully attack on the bridge. While Mya discusses her writing with Mrs. Braxton, the bullies belittle Steven. Fortunately for Steven, Mya anticipated this and makes a plan to beat the bullies at their own game.	Students identify with Mya's concern for Steven's welfare. They see that she feels responsible for his predicament. She was not able to warn him in time. They notice her uneasiness as she tries to make a plan while listening to Mrs. Braxton's good news about her writing.	Students need a copy of the text. It can be read aloud to students, or they can read it silently. Small groups can also read together.	Mya must have learned a thing or two from Mrs. Chinkley because she uses a bluff to distract Bonnita and Franka.	Taking the bridge was pretty symbolic for Mya. She was also taking back her power. Mrs. Chinkley was first to get the ball rolling. She began helping the girl rebuild her confidence. Meowy and Momma also made her feel loved again.
ussion stions	These questions encourage students to explain why Mya felt responsible for Steven's welfare, what Mrs. Braxton was thinking when she read over Mya's paper, and why faking a joke about Franka and Bonnita actually worked.	Students begin to realize that bullies can be defeated at their own game.	Students need the discussion questions and a copy of the text to look for the answers. There is an opportunity for open dialogue among students in the form of large group conversations.	Bullies have weaknesses just like everyone else. They are human. They can be dealt with. It helps to have a "partner-in-crime" and a determination to succeed.	The bullies attacked Steven for two reasons: he was breaking their rules and he was Mya's friend. Mya anticipated this. She planned ahead for this situation and was ready when it came. Being prepared is half the battle when dealing with bullies.
vity 1: erving nal	Students create a journal filled with deserving thoughts. They change their lives through daily writings about things they deserve. There are only two activities in this unit because the journal entries extend over four weeks.	Students will realize that thoughts are very powerful and written thoughts are even more powerful.	Students make a blank notebook. Over a four-week period, they write deserving thoughts using prompts from an idea bank. These thoughts will bring about change.	The power of positive thinking and envisioning a future of joy and success combine to make dreams come true.	Students can change their paths, especially if they are heading on a downward spiral. When the mind envisions what we want for ourselves, these things manifest themselves. It is the power of intent.
vity 2: bration	Students look through their journals to read what they have written. They decide how much their confidence has grown. They notice changes.	Students conclude that changes have taken place through daily journaling. They accept that they are deserving of all the good that life has to offer.	Students flip through their journals and write a summary of the changes they have observed. The class gathers to share insights.	Sharing and hearing demonstrations of growth is inspiring.	Students make big changes with this activity. Their confidence and sense of worth skyrockets.

STEVEN GETS EVEN

It was nearly recess time on a day that would prove to be very eventful for both Mya and Steven. The morning had gone by smoothly. The afternoon was about to begin.

Mya handed in her math work and then she passed by her new neighbor's desk. She noticed that Steven seemed to be settling in quite well. It looked like he'd been part of the class for a long time. His desk was packed with books, papers, and notebooks, and most of these were sticking out from underneath the lid of the desk.

She made a mental note to help him organize one day, but now it was time to get her coat. Recess was about to begin. Mya got in line behind Steven. She promised herself to stick with him no matter what. She anticipated an attack and planned to back him up or stand with him during the ambush.

But before she could warn Steven not to go on the playground's bridge, Mrs. Braxton called Mya over to her desk. The kids went outside with Mrs. Fiedler's class. Steven went with them. Mya's worried eyes followed him out the door.

Mrs. Braxton started talking to Mya about her book report. She began by telling her that she had read it over a few days ago, but Mya heard none of the teacher's words. Mya's mind was on the playground where she knew Steven was going to be pushed to the limit. She was certain it was starting at that very moment.

"You know, Mya, your report is very good," Mrs. Braxton said. "Most of the class just rewrote the story in their own words. They didn't really think about the message, like you did." She went on, "Your writing is actually an opinion paper. You try to let your reader see bullies as you do. It appears that you know quite a bit about bullies and have very strong feelings about the main character in the book. I am impressed with your mature writing. I don't understand why you were so afraid to read it. You knew very well that it was finished but you pretended it wasn't."

Mya just shrugged her shoulders. She couldn't tell Mrs. Braxton her inner feelings. She didn't know her well enough. She felt most teachers weren't to be trusted, anyway. She couldn't tell the woman that she was afraid to read because of the bullies. If she mentioned that Bonnita and Franka were bullying her, she'd look like a tattletale. Then her problems would definitely get worse. If the bullies got a whiff that she tattled on them, she would never hear the end of it. Besides teachers are adults and don't know how to deal with kids' problems. They don't understand their worries and feelings, even though they were once young themselves. How could she explain what was really upsetting her?

Of course, she knew why she couldn't read to the class. She did not want to give the bullies another chance to ridicule her. She was picked on enough. She did not wish for more abuse as a result of her report. The whole class would probably laugh at her work because it was so different from theirs. She couldn't take that risk. The classroom wasn't a safe place for her. She was too new to have supporters. In truth, Mya felt her report wasn't good enough. It didn't sound like the other reports.

Her mind wandered back to the playground. Her face took on a far away

look. She wondered what the bullies were up to at this very moment.

Mrs. Braxton noticed her nervousness. "Is something wrong, Mya?" She saw Mya's eyes look toward the door. "O-O-Oh, I will let you go out in a minute." She then went on, "If you don't mind, I would like to teach the class how to write an opinion paper like yours. May I use your work as a model for the class to copy?"

Mya was shocked. If the class knew that the teacher liked her work so much, she would be a total outcast. In her mind, she could hear them belittling her.

"Oh, no, Mrs. Braxton! You can't do that. I-I-I'd be too embarrassed!" cried Mya.

"But Mya, there is nothing to be embarrassed about. This is exactly what the class needs to learn. Let's think about this and talk about it again soon. Now get going, or you'll miss recess," Mrs. Braxton said. She rushed Mya out the door.

As she walked down the hall, Mya started thinking about Mrs. Braxton's suggestion, but she knew she had to go rescue Steven. Suddenly she stopped in her tracks and darted back into the classroom.

Mrs. Braxton looked up with a questioning look on her face. With the hint of a tiny smile, Mya said, "Yes, but don't tell them it is mine! Can we keep it a secret?" She realized she should take some pride in that paper instead of just feeling embarrassed about it. After all, Mrs. Braxton thought it was good enough to use as a model. But she had an intervention to take care of at this moment and rushed out to the playground before Mrs. Braxton could even answer.

As she predicted, trouble was already brewing on the playground. She noticed a huge crowd at the base of the ladder to the bridge. All the kids were looking upward toward the porthole. There on the hanging bridge, above the crowd, was Steven. His head was down and his shoulders looked slumped. He was standing alone and looking very sad.

Mya realized that those slumped shoulders meant a weakened Steven, a tormented Steven, and probably an abused Steven. She bumped her way through the crowd and crawled up the ladder to see what was happening. The whole group took in a big breath when they saw where Mya was going. They knew that eventually she would pay for what she was doing.

Franka was at the top of the ladder, poking her head through the porthole. Bonnita was right behind her. Their heads were bobbing as vile, degrading words poured out of their mouths. They were calling Steven horrible, nasty names and were belittling him as they had done to her.

Mya was on a mission to save Steven and no one could stop her. In her hurry to get through the porthole, she stepped on both of Bonnita's new white sneakers and made a big smudge on each toe. That made Bonnita squeal and quickly move out of Mya's way. Bonnita yelled to Mya, "You

are going to be so sorry you did that!" But Bonnita's threat didn't stop Mya. She forged on.

She elbowed Franka in the ribs and Franka let out a pitiful scream as she whined, "You bully! Who do you think you are? The teacher will hear about this!" Then she whimpered and began to cry like a baby. Mya secretly chuckled when she heard Franka call *her* a bully. She felt some enjoyment when she made the real bullies cry.

Mya had easily pushed herself past Bonnita and then Franka. She popped up onto the bridge to stand with Steven against the enemy. As she walked over to him, she thought about Mrs. Chinkley's trick to stop Franka from taking her job at the market. When Mya got by Steven's side, she cupped her hand up to his ear, pointed back to the girls at the top of the ladder, and whispered something. He began to smile at her. She smiled back to him and then they both started to laugh hysterically, as if they had just shared a great joke. They laughed for quite a few minutes and finally the crowd turned their eyes toward the two girls. Bonnita and Franka looked stunned and backed themselves down the ladder. They pushed their way over to a nearby bench and sat down together. They wrapped their arms around each other and blubbered over what had just taken place.

Then suddenly, as if they practiced, Steven and Mya walked over to the middle of the bridge and sat down cross-legged. This reminded Mya of the last time she was on the bridge, when she did almost the same exact thing. But today, there was laughter instead of tears in her eyes. This time, she felt lighthearted because she had a friend who gave her courage to stand up against the bullies.

Next, they went over to the opening where the slide was. They looked down. There was a crowd of students looking up at them. Laughter and giggles came from the group below them. Mya and Steven began motioning to their classmates to come up and enjoy the bridge with them.

Slowly, one-by-one, the other students felt brave and climbed up the ladder. Some walked right past Franka and Bonnita in defiance. Dozens of happy kids scrambled across the bridge and down the slippery slide at the other end, laughing and screaming. They acted as if it was something they were used to doing everyday.

Bonnita and Franka just glared at all of them in disbelief.

Who would have thought that Steven, who looked so timid, would give Mya such courage? Together they withstood the demeaning words. Together they were as brave as knights.

Where they were, they could not even see the girls and they almost forgot how badly they were treated. They knew it was risky but together they defied the monsters. They decided to be strong and fight back. It worked!

Mya, the girl who had been bullied herself, stood by Steven without a second thought. No one else had the courage, but she did! She had done a very brave thing to stand by him at risk to herself. Somehow Steven made her feel courageous. She remembered reading about General George Washington who took Trenton away from the British bullies. She felt just like George that day. They took the bridge!

The two of them stayed on that bridge for the rest of recess, guarding against further bully attacks. They seemed to enjoy winning the bridge for the rest of the class. It was good getting even with bullies and all it took was a whisper, a smile, a pointed finger, and lots of defiant laughter.

On their way back into the classroom, Mya and Steven brought up the rear of the line. Billy Bonner, a curious boy ahead of them asked Mya, "What did you say to Steven that was so funny? Did you make a joke about Franka or something?"

Mya just looked at Steven and smiled as she said, "Oh, that's a secret." She winked at Steven as the two of them just laughed over the fact that there was no joke at all. She had just told him to smile and then laugh really loud and hard. Then she pointed at the bullies to make it look like they were enjoying a joke about them. It was all a bluff, but it worked. The bridge had been taken back.

Steven Gets Even

Discussion Questions

 Why did Mya feel responsible for protecting Steven on the playground?

 Mrs. Braxton was an interesting teacher. She realized Mya was a fabulous writer and a very deep thinker, unlike most of her students. What clues proved Mrs. Braxton believed Mya was not an ordinary student?

 Mya and Steven defeated the bullies by pretense. They faked a bully-joke and humiliated the girls in front of the class. Why did this tactic work? When had a bluff stopped them before?

Deserving Journal

In this activity you will be making your own journal. This journal will be filled with daily entries that explain what you deserve in your life. These writings will declare that you are worthy of all the good life has to offer.

Mya felt that she and Steven deserved to be able to play on the bridge. She also decided that everyone in her class was worthy enough to enjoy the bridge as well. That is why she stood up against the bullies and defeated them.

If Mya had a *Deserving Journal*, she would have felt confident enough to stand up to the bullies every time they attacked. Her writings would have given her a bold, courageous outlook on life. After creating this journal, she would definitely not have refused to read her report to the class.

Making a journal like this can change your life. Instead of being a victim, you will feel strong. It will give you the pride and confidence you deserve. As time moves on, your feelings of worthiness will strengthen.

Here are your tasks:

- Staple together 5 sheets of paper inside two pieces of light cardboard (front and back) for the cover.

- Decorate the cover with drawings and write *Deserving Journal* in bold letters. Add your name.

- Inside the journal, enter the dates (four to a page) covering a four-week period. Space them out so you have room to write under each date. **Use the example on the next page to help you.**

- Under each date, write what you deserve everyday for a whole month. To get you started, there are some ideas in the *Idea Bank*.

- Use one of the sentences to begin your deserving statements. You can repeat the ones you like best. Just remember to add details to your entry. The more details you add, the more meaningful the statement.

- Place this journal in a special place or on a shelf. Since you will work on it everyday for a whole month, you will want to protect it from loss and damage.

Journal page examples:

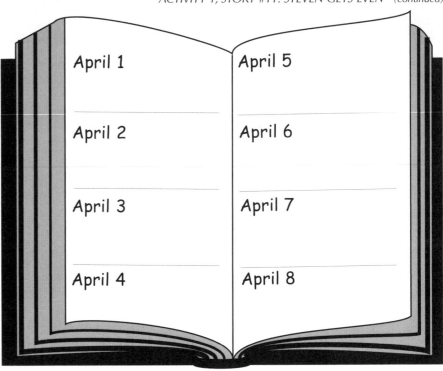

April 1	April 5
April 2	April 6
April 3	April 7
April 4	April 8

IDEA BANK		
I deserve to be happy.	I deserve to be smart.	I deserve to do well in school.
I deserve to be confident.	I deserve to feel accepted.	I deserve to have many friends.
I deserve to feel strong.	I deserve to enjoy life.	I deserve to get good grades.
I deserve to be treated fairly.	I deserve to be respected.	I deserve to like myself.
I deserve to be trusted.	I deserve to be free from worry.	I deserve to accept others.

Here is an example for April 1:

April 1: I deserve to be smart. I do everything I can to get good grades. I study hard, I do my homework, and I pay attention in class. My mother says I am going to be a doctor one day. I put my heart and soul into my schoolwork and I deserve to be smart.

Celebration Day

At the end of a month, celebrate the completion your *Deserving Journal*. On this day, leaf through your journal very carefully. You will be amazed at what you have written and how your feelings of confidence have grown. Take notice of the wonderful changes that have begun to happen.

Then flip to the back of the journal and date your last entry. Write down everything that has changed for the better because of your new feelings of worthiness. Tell what you have noticed, no matter how small. You may simply list things or put them in paragraph form. Write in detail explaining the changes.

To make this event more special, join your classmates in a circle and talk about the changes you have noticed.

Discuss these questions:

- How has your confidence grown?

- How do you feel differently about your life?

- In what ways do you accept yourself more?

- How has your attitude about school changed?

- In what ways are you better able to handle difficulties?

Unit 12:

RUMORS

STORY #12 SUMMARY

Something Strange

The bullies, Bonnita and Franka, spread lying gossip about Mya. They create a rumor that she is a cat killer. Somehow they know about Meowy and the fishhook. Steven stands behind Mya and she plans to retaliate.

on	Objectives	Student Goals	Materials and Lesson	Insights	Author's Message
#12 **·thing ·ge**	Students understand how rumors impact a person when they see how a terrible untruth devastates Mya.	Students identify with Mya's despair as she hears that Franka and Bonnita have spread a lie about her. Mya is devastated when she hears that the bullies have said that she is a cat killer. Students notice the strength Steven gives Mya as he promises to stand by her.	Students need a copy of the text. It can be read aloud to students, or they can read it silently. Small groups can also read together.	The question is, how did the bullies get hold of the information about Meowy and the fishhook? Mya never mentioned this to anyone, not even Steven.	Students come to realize that it is criminal to tell lies about people just to turn others against them. It does no good. No one ever looks up to those who gossip.
·ssion ·tions	These questions encourage students to explain why Steven remained faithful to Mya even when warned to abandon her. They imagine what was going through Mya's mind as she heard the rumor. They think back about how she would have reacted at the beginning of the story.	Students attempt to see Mya in a different light. Even though she is upset over the rumor, she still is able to handle it.	Students need the discussion questions and a copy of the text to look for the answers. There is an opportunity for open dialogue among students in the form of large group conversations.	Mya has grown emotionally. She doesn't react by crying when she hears what new problems the bullies have caused for her. Rather, she has a cool determination to get to the truth.	This chapter signifies a big change in Mya. Bolstered by Steven's support and feeling more confident, she is determined to defeat the bullies once and for all.
·ty 1: ·Play ·p	Students play the game *Gossip* to understand how gossip "spreaders" change rumors as they are retold.	Students conclude that people don't listen very well. They interpret information differently as they restate the facts.	Students need a copy of the worksheet. They first form a large circle and play the game. Afterward, students draw conclusions as to why the gossip changed. They discuss their opinions.	The intent of gossip is to harm the person about whom it is being spread. It is rare that it is not embellished as people repeat it. "Gossipers" will most likely enhance the gossip to make it worse.	This activity encourages students to realize that gossip is cruel and insidious. It changes the truth to meet the needs of the listener.
·ty 2: ·p ·ssions	Students consider the ramifications of gossip.	Students realize that the spread of gossip is harmful to the person it disrespects. They develop their own opinions and relate facts as they discuss a particular question.	Students need the worksheet and a pencil. Teams of four select a question and present their opinions to the class. Their goal is to convince the class to believe as they do.	Gossip has no place in classrooms or elsewhere in our daily life. The fact that it is embellished for shock value convinces us this is so.	This activity is aimed at encouraging students to think deeply about the influence gossip has on peoples' reputations. Gossip directs what we believe about people. The worse it is, the faster it spreads.
·ty 3: ·the ·p	Students form a *Stop the Gossip Club*. Its goal is to end the spread of vicious rumors once and for all.	Students work together to develop a club whose sole purpose is to end gossip. They brainstorm ways to stop listening and repeating gossip. They attempt to convince others to end the habit.	Students need the worksheet, a pencil, and time to brainstorm ways to end gossip.	We must refuse to spread gossip, refuse to listen to it, and refuse to take joy in the pain of others.	Gossip is more than just rumors. Our society condones it. Tabloid newspapers thrive on gossip. It is a bully tactic. It must stop.
·ty 4: ·a ·act	Students develop a contract for their club. They use ideas from the chart in Activity 3 to create a contract.	Students include information from the previous activity to develop a contract. The sample guides their planning.	Students need the worksheet and a pencil. Once they have listed the ways to end gossip, they design a contract, sign it, and become ambassadors to end the spread of gossip.	The contract is a message for all who see it. Gossip must be stopped.	No matter how innocent the gossip, it is wrong. No one has the right to criticize or spread rumors about another. Gossip actually reflects the spreaders' weaknesses. It reveals their lack of self worth.

SOMETHING STRANGE

It was another cold winter morning, and just a few days after taking the bridge. She shivered off the dampness as she walked up the stairs to her classroom. Thinking it would be a typical day she readied herself for school. Mya never suspected that things might turn on her. She took her backpack over to her desk as usual, sat on her chair, and spread her homework out. Suddenly, she sensed something strange in the air and scanned the room looking for what was different.

Groups of kids were clustered around as usual. But they were looking straight at her, whispering behind their hands, and pointing. Their looks were accusatory and she knew something was up. She raised her eyebrows, shrugged her shoulders, and got up to take her bag out to her locker. As she passed one of the smaller groups of girls clustered near the door, one of them said, "Shame on you. How could you do such a thing?"

Mya must have had a confused look on her face because Zoey Lawrence, who up until now had hardly ever spoken to Mya said, "Don't you like cats? They are precious creatures that deserve to live just like we do. How could you?"

Mya was really puzzled now. She was stumped by the question Zoey asked about cats. What was she talking about? Her mind raced as she continued out the door to her locker. She wished it would all just go away. She wanted it all to be a bad dream.

Out in the hall, she saw Steven coming up the stairs and heading to his locker. When he saw the look on Mya's face, he ran over to her. "What's wrong," he asked? "Are you feeling all right?"

Mya quickly blurted out what Zoey had said. She mentioned that she didn't have a clue as to what it was all about. Just then a couple of boys pulled Steven toward the boy's bathroom.

"You shouldn't be friends with a cat killer," said Leonard Miller as he grabbed Steven's arm. "It just might rub off on you," Leonard continued. "You can't afford to have a friend like that. You're too new. She is an embarrassment to this classroom and if you hang around with her, people will shun you too."

As Steven was pulled into the washroom, he turned toward Mya and mouthed, "I'll find out. Don't worry." He went in with the boys. Mya just stood by her locker holding her book bag and waited. In her heart she knew that the news would be bad. What did Leonard mean, cat killer?

When Steven came back, he walked straight over to Mya, not paying attention to the warning from the boys. He had a worried look on his face. He said, "Well Mya, it's a really wild story. You are not going to believe this. They think you killed a cat by leaving a fishhook in its mouth. Where do they get this stuff? They said that the hook got all corroded with rust and then the cat got an infection. Leonard said that you never bothered to help the poor animal and left it to die. The cat wasn't able to eat and it starved to death. What will they think of next? Boy, can those girls tell a whopper!" He shook his head as he finished the story.

Mya's mind was spinning and then she asked, "What girls, Bonnita and Franka?"

"Of course," he said with a scowl on his face. "Who else could come up with something that stupid?"

She knew about rumors. They were never forgotten. If they were especially bad, rumors followed you forever. The story follows you through every grade and kids that don't even know you will remind you of the rumor. And worse than that, they are usually all big, bad lies.

"Steven, you don't believe a word of it, do you?" she asked him.

"Of course not, Mya. No one would do anything that mean to a helpless animal, not even Bonnita and Franka," he added with a sarcastic laugh.

Bonnita and Franka were out to get Mya again but this time they'd gone too far. She suddenly realized that she had probably outsmarted them way too many times and they didn't like it one bit. They were desperately searching for something horrible to say about Mya. With this rumor, they had found a way to turn the whole class against her and were also out to make Steven hate her.

Mya was not about to stand still for this. She knew they were implying that Meowy was dead because of the fishhook. That was definitely not true! Momma had removed the whole fishhook. Mya saw it with her own eyes, didn't she? And she saw Momma use anti-germ cream, just to make sure there would be no infection. She had spoken to Bobby Blanko. She remembered telling him to take Meowy to the vet to get her lip checked. She scratched her head. She thought she had done all the right things. Now Mya began doubting herself. What if they were right?

And what puzzled her most was how in the world they found out about Meowy's fishhook. She concluded that those girls went to extremes to hurt people.

No, she knew Meowy was alive and well, even though she had not seen her since the day she and her mom saved the cat. Mya's mind drifted back and forth for a few moments, thinking the bullies were big liars who enjoyed spreading venom like snakes. Then she would doubt her belief that the cat was still alive. She couldn't

wait for the school day to end so she could prove that Meowy was not infected, not sick, and NOT DEAD!

Steven looked at Mya with a worried look on his face. He said, "Mya, I know you didn't kill any cat! I want to let you know that I will stand by you no matter what. If I can do anything to help you, just let me know. Now, let's go into the classroom together and stare down those liars."

Mya already felt better, just to know that someone supported her.

They put their book bags in their lockers and shut the doors. They walked proudly into the room, shoulder-to-shoulder. They were ready for whatever stares came their way.

Something Strange

Discussion Questions

 Why did Steven go directly over to Mya, ignoring the boys' warnings about hanging around with a person who would kill a cat?

 There were probably many emotions going through Mya's mind as she listened to the rumors being spread about her. Perhaps there was worry, anger, and doubt. But also she felt confident. Explain the reasons behind all these fluctuating emotions.

 Mya was obviously a lot stronger now, compared to the way she reacted to the bullies at the beginning of the story. Tell how you know she had become a more powerful person. In contrast, tell how she would have reacted if this had happened at the beginning of the story.

Let's Play Gossip

People usually gossip about someone they know. Often the gossip is mean-spirited, like Franka's. She wanted the class to believe that Mya was a cat killer even when she knew it was a big lie.

In this activity, the class will play the game, *Gossip*. First, you'll need to form a large circle. The teacher will begin the game by whispering some gossip (something that no one knows) to the first person in the circle. Each student then passes the gossip by whispering it from one person to the next. In this game, spread positive gossip rather than the kind Franka started.

Once the gossip moves around the circle to the end, the last person must stand up and repeat the gossip to everyone. The teacher writes the statement on the board. Then the class compares it to the original gossip. Look for any differences in the message as the speakers and the listeners changed it. This change comes about because, as people repeat gossip in their own words, they often exaggerate or change the message to make it more interesting. The more extensive the rumor, the easier the facts become confused.

Discuss what happened to the gossip in your gossip circle. Here is your task:

■ Talk about what was originally said.

■ Tell where you were in the circle and what you heard.

■ Explain what you told the next person.

■ Compare the original to the final statement.

■ At the end, draw a conclusion about what you think caused the gossip to change as it moved around the circle. Did it become more exaggerated? Why did this happen.

■ Tell how you feel about gossip.

Gossip Discussions

ACTIVITY 2, STORY #12: SOMETHING STRANGE

In this activity, the class will divide into teams of four, to discuss gossip. Each team will prepare to explain its thoughts about one of the following questions. All of them relate to gossip and the injuries caused by its spread. The teams must back up their answers with proof from the story and from real life. The groups then present to the class.

Here are your questions:

- Did Franka tell a lie about Mya in the beginning? Then, as it spread through the classroom, did it continue to be mean-spirited, and get worse? Tell how this happened.

- Could Mya's classmates be the ones at fault? Could they have changed the gossip from the truth to a lie as it was spread? Is it their fault, rather than Franka's, that people believed Mya was a cat killer? What is your opinion of this?

- Why did people turn against Mya and believe the worst about her?

- Why didn't the boys side with Mya and Steven against Franka? Why did they warn Steven to stay away from Mya?

- Why do people gossip? Why do people enjoy spreading it?

- Is gossip ever a good thing? How do you think gossiping got started?

- When you hear gossip about someone, what makes you interested in it?

- If you gossip about others, are you a bad person?

- If you heard gossip about a friend, would you stop it? How would you do that?

- Gossiping, unfortunately, is fun to do, especially when it makes others look bad. Why does gossiping about the failures of others make you feel better about yourself?

- How does gossip hurt peoples' reputations? Does anyone have the right to gossip?

- Do magazines and newspapers ever publish gossip or do they always tell the truth about people?

- Is gossip a way of judging someone before they have a chance to defend themselves?

- Are television news programs just gossip or the truth?

Stop The Gossip Club

ACTIVITY 3, STORY #12: SOMETHING STRANGE

Now is your chance to create a *Stop the Gossip Club*! Gossip and rumors are hurtful things and it is time to refuse to be judgmental about others. We must stop taking joy in the misfortunes of friends and those we may not like as much. Mya's class should have done this activity before the cat killer rumor spread.

As a class, brainstorm ideas that will act as guides to teach people how to stop mean-spirited gossip in its tracks. Think of ways to empower people to refuse to listen to gossip and never start it or pass it onto others. Add ideas to stop those who are not members of the club from passing rumors on to you. Perhaps you will simply walk away. Maybe you will lecture gossipers on the pain they cause.

To begin, brainstorm a list of things people can do to stop listening, repeating, or starting hurtful gossip.

Use the chart below to put down your ideas.

How Can We Stop Listening to Gossip?	How Can We Stop Repeating Gossip?	How Can We Convince Others to Stop Gossiping?

Make a Contract

ACTIVITY 4, STORY #12: SOMETHING STRANGE

In this activity, your class will design its own contract for your *Stop The Gossip Club*. In order to be a member, you must sign the contract and uphold its message. On the next page there is a sample contract. Use it as a guide.

Your task will be to design your own contract using the ideas selected from Activity 3.

Here's what to do:

■ Rejoin your team from Activity 2.

■ On large chart paper, use a marker to create your sample contract.

■ All groups must then display their contracts to the whole class and argue their value.

■ The class then votes on the best choice.

■ Once one is adopted, all students may sign it.

■ Individual versions can be handed out to members so they can have their own contract copies.

■ The teams then design anti-gossip posters to be displayed in the classroom.

Once signed, hang the contract in the room for all to see. Each signer will officially be a lifetime member of the *Stop the Gossip Club*. The class will be ambassadors on the mission to end rumor mills around the school and beyond.

MEMBERSHIP CONTRACT

Stop The Gossip Club

This document officially certifies that (printed name of joining member)

_____ is a member in good

standing of the *Stop the Gossip Club*. This club was established at

(school's name) _____ ,

in room _____ on (date)_____ .

As a member of this club, I promise to stop gossip in its tracks.
I will do everything in my power to:

- Ignore gossip
- Interrupt it when it is being spread
- Stop gossip in its tracks by using the official stop the gossip hand signal
  (raising my hand like a stop sign)
- Walk away from gossipers
- Refuse to listen to rumors
- Refuse to add information to rumors
- Refuse to take enjoyment in the misfortune of others

(Place your right hand on your heart) I pledge to faithfully continue to spread
the message that gossip and rumors only serve to hurt people. As a member of
this club, it is my duty never to take enjoyment in the misfortune of those who
cannot defend themselves.

The gossip stops here!

Signed _____

Date _____

THE PLAN

STORY #13 SUMMARY

Mya's Mission

Mya develops a plan to prove the bullies wrong. She decides to get Meowy from Bobby Blanko to show everyone that the animal is alive. She runs into a problem, however. Meowy has been taken to the SPCA.

Lesson	Objectives	Student Goals	Materials and Lesson	Insights	Author's Message
Story #13 **Mya's Mission**	Students learn that Mya plans to find Meowy to prove her innocence. She runs into a slight problem, however. Meowy is at the SPCA. Students are inspired by Mya's motivation to clear her reputation.	Students discover Mya's goal. She plans to show the class how deceitful, disrespectful, and uncaring the bullies are.	Students need a copy of the text. It can be read aloud to students, or they can read it silently. Small groups can also read together.	Mya sets her goal to stop the bullies from controlling her life. She realizes she has more in common with them than she suspected. She does not wish to follow in their footsteps.	The bullies have gone too far. They have lied to turn the class against Mya. Her goal is to teach the class that people must stand up to bullying. As her own advocate, she makes a plan to end the tyranny. She has a backbone and she is about to use it. She is proud of her treatment of Meowy and it is time everyone knows that.
Discussion Questions	These questions encourage students to think about why Bonnita and Franka continue to harass Mya, what enjoyment the bullies get by humiliating Mya, and what steps a person should take to stop bullies in their tracks.	Students identify with Mya's plight as she plans to prove the bullies wrong. She sets out on her mission to catch them in a bold-faced lie.	Students need the discussion questions and a copy of the text to look for the answers. There is an opportunity for open dialogue among students in the form of large group conversations.	Mya has begun to like herself more and more. Self-acceptance is a powerful thing. It has motivated her to go after the lie and stop it before her reputation is destroyed.	In a way, the gossip was a gift to Mya. It forced her to end the abuse. In fact, she could now see herself as a confident, powerful, clever girl, who is worthy of respect.
Activity 1: **Make A Plan**	Students plan for a situation in which a fellow student cheats by copying a science paper. Instead of discovering the cheater, students are wrongly accused of cheating.	Students identify with Mya's plight as they are (hypothetically) accused of cheating. They are directed to develop a plan to catch the thief to save their reputations.	Students need a pencil, a copy of the worksheet, and time to fill in the charts with lists of ideas they would use to catch a liar.	Cheating goes on in schools and in every aspect of today's life. Morality and truth seem to be choices not rules. Students believe that it is acceptable to tell their version of truth. As a society, we must realize that everyone has to be accountable.	No matter what, the truth is always the path we must choose. Perhaps that is why there are so many lessons about the truth in literature. When reputations are at stake, the truth must prevail.
Activity 2: **Detective Work**	Students collect ideas on chart paper to accumulate ways to capture cheaters.	Students realize that it is good to have a plan for catching cheaters.	Students need the worksheet and a pencil to jot down their ideas. Volunteers fill in the charts to organize the ideas brought out by the class. The charts, from the previous activity, offer the best ways to catch a thief.	Sometimes it is better to solve a problem collectively. Often it leads us to make better choices.	Students will have the opportunity to compare their detective work and draw the best conclusions for catching a cheater.
Activity 3: **Beat the Cheater**	Students analyze the chart made in the previous activity to decide which ideas would be the strongest for catching a cheater. They then write an essay arguing why these ideas would be most effective.	Students focus ways to catch a cheater. Their goal is to go with what would be most successful as they make their decisions.	Students need the worksheet, a pencil, time to analyze ideas, and paper to compose an essay. They argue the best choices. Their goal is to gather supportive evidence to catch a cheater. They read the essays aloud and score them with the *Grading Rubric for Speeches* from Activity 4, Unit 6.	Our reputation is something we must nurture, develop, and protect as we mature. It is the image we portray in society. It is not a static thing and its development begins in grade school.	We are not perfect beings and we often make poor choices. This activity allows students to imagine what it would be like to be falsely accused. They see how complicated it can be to catch a liar.

MYA'S MISSION

That Monday turned out to be "Black Monday," the worst school day of Mya's life. It was such a terrible day for Mya that she even forgot it was her eleventh birthday. Time dragged and dragged and the clock barely ticked away the hours. Steven continued to give her encouraging smiles whenever he saw her looking depressed. He made her feel as if she wasn't alone.

Finally the last bell rang and Mya practically flew off the school grounds. She knew she was on a very important mission. She had to prove the bullies were totally wrong, once and for all. She was through with them. She also had to reveal to the class exactly how mean and hateful they were.

She was determined to teach the class that people should stand up to bullies. She wanted everyone to know that bullies' lies are hurtful and they destroy lives. When people are bullied they change. They become weak and miserable.

She decided, sadly, that she had a lot in common with the bullies. All three of them had a dislike for themselves and hoped no one would ever find out. The bullies covered their weaknesses by being mean to other people and Mya covered hers by simply ignoring them. But now she was beginning to feel that it was time she stood up for herself and proved once and for all, that she was not someone to mess with. She had to show the bullies that she had a backbone. Her reputation was at stake. Her self-respect had almost been destroyed. She must prove that she was worthy of her classmates' acceptance and that she was not someone who could be abused and mistreated ever again.

When bullies get together, they try to make others feel bad about themselves with lies, biting words, and rumors. While Mya was fearful and worried that Franka and Bonnita would continue these attacks, she liked herself too much to let them ruin her life. She had a lesson to teach them. She decided right then and there that she was not going to be like them ever again.

As usual, on her way home from school, she stopped at the produce market. Mrs. Chinkley saw that something was wrong and Mya told her about the events that had happened that day. She said she was on a mission to stop the tormenting once and for all. She even told her the true story about the cat incident.

Mrs. Chinkley gave Mya a high-five and said, "Good for you! If I can help, let me know. I support you and I know that you will succeed because you are a very good person. If your class really knew you, they would never believe that you could be a cat killer."

Mya smiled and gave Mrs. Chinkley a big hug. She had grown very fond of this wonderful, loving woman. She asked if she could go home instead of work at the market that day. She was on a mission to redeem her reputation. Mrs. Chinkley hugged her, brushed Mya's hair back, and put her hat on her head.

"Good luck, Honey. I know things will work out just fine for you," she said. Then she scooted Mya out the door, dropping a banana and a pear in her coat pocket. "These are for extra energy," she said with a smile. As she watched Mya leave, she walked to the back of the store and reached for the phone. She began pressing buttons.

Mya went straight to her landlord's house first. It wasn't far from her house. If anyone knew where Meowy was, it was Bobby Blanko. Meowy was his cat, after all. If she could prove the cat was still

alive, she could stop the rumors. All she had to do was find the cat.

Bobby answered the door. He was working on his homework at the dining room table. She said, "Hi Bobby, where's Meowy? I need to find her, it is really important, and you have to tell me!" Mya's words exploded out of her mouth like popcorn popping in a bag, but Bobby just looked at her. His words were not the ones she wanted to hear.

"She's gone," Bobby said. "My dad took her to the SPCA a few days ago." Bobby's eyes looked sad.

Mya's thoughts zeroed in on what the letters SPCA, meant. She said out loud, "Do you mean the Society for the Prevention of Cruelty to Animals? Is that the place where people take unwanted cats and dogs for adoption?"

"Yes," Bobby answered. "Dad said that he didn't need a cat that got into things and caused a lot of expensive veterinary bills," Bobby looked down. His whole body looked sad. Mya could tell the cat was probably Bobby's only and best friend and he was missing her a lot. That gave her more reason to find Meowy.

"Quick, get your bike, Bobby," she called as she ran out the door.

"Where are we going?" Bobby asked.

"We have some saving to do. We are going to rescue a poor defenseless animal and save a girl who deserves to be treated right," she said powerfully.

Discussion Questions

 Mya's mission was to reveal to the class how evil Bonnita and Franka were. What do you suppose caused these girls to attack Mya so cruelly for as long as they did?

 The class believed the gossip that Mya was a cat killer. How did Bonnita and Franka feel about this?

 When bullies succeed, they gain power and that power causes them to go on bullying. What steps should a person take to stop bullies?

Make A Plan

Mya was on a mission. She had to save her reputation. It had all but been destroyed by Franka's lie and she made a plan to retrieve it.

Imagine that you have a similar problem. Pretend you have been accused of cheating on a science test. The rumor that you copied someone's answers is floating around your classroom. The evidence proves that you cheated because on both test papers, the answers are word-for-word exact. Your answers look erased, smudged, and rewritten.

The truth is that a student saw your answers when the papers were piled on the teacher's desk. She knew you always studied hard. When no one was looking, she copied your answers and smudged your paper to make it look like you changed your answers to match hers. Your reputation is at stake. You have always been an honest person. How will you prove the cheater is at fault?

You are now on a mission. Your task is to write out your plan to expose the cheater. You must save your reputation.

Think about:
- Ways to catch her cheating again
- Proving your answers were copied at the teacher's desk
- Finding witnesses
- Getting help to destroy this rumor
- The kind of detective work you will use to catch her "red-handed"
- The cheater's past history of lying

Write out your plan on the lines below:

Detective Work

In this activity your class will do some detective work. As a group, your goal is to come to with the best ways to catch a cheater. You will be taking notes as a group, based on the information and suggestions from the previous activity. Put up four large pieces of chart paper. Have four volunteers label the charts using the headings below. As the class volunteers ideas, the note takers will write them on these charts fitting them in the proper category.

Possible Suspect Behaviors

Best Ways to Catch the Cheater

Evidence

Best Ways to Prove Your Innocence

Beat the Cheater

ACTIVITY 3, STORY #13: MYA'S MISSION

Using the information gathered in Activity 2, pick the best ideas. Look for those that would definitely stop a cheater from cheating.

Next, write an *opinion paper* that describes which ideas you feel would be most successful. Your goal is to beat a cheater. Use the suggestions below to plan your essay.

■ Which actions will best save your reputation in the classroom?

■ Explain how you will gather evidence. The evidence must prove who the cheater is, without a doubt.

■ Demonstrate ways to show you are honest and truthful, and would never cheat on a test.

■ Tell how you will catch the liar red-handed.

With power in your voice and a clear and forceful message, practice rereading your opinion paper until you are comfortable with it. When the essays are completed and practiced, use the *Grading Rubric for Speeches*, Activity 4, page 87, to score the essays as they are read aloud. As a result of hearing these essays, there will be no cheating in your classroom.

Unit 14:

THERE'S A SMALL PROBLEM

STORY #14 SUMMARY

At the SPCA

Mya runs into a problem when she tries to rescue Meowy. She almost tells a lie but someone special turns up to save the day. Then there is the eleventh birthday surprise that changes lives. The bonding and empowering that goes on in this episode, warms the heart.

Lesson	Objectives	Student Goals	Materials and Lesson	Insights	Author's Message
Story #14 **At the SPCA**	Students read about Mya and Bobby as they arrive at the SPCA to reclaim Meowy. They understand Mya's frustration and desperate attempt as she almost lies to acquire the cat.	Students see Mya's fear of losing the cat to a stranger. They feel her anguish as she attempts to prove that Franka and Bonnita spread the lies about her. They celebrate when a miracle happens.	Students need a copy of the text. It can be read aloud to students, or they can read it silently. Small groups can also read together.	Mya is a clever, determined girl. Out of desperation, she will do anything to get the cat and save her reputation. She finally has belief in herself. Nothing will stop her from accomplishing her goal. Good comes from good.	Mya realizes that ᵗ is a connection between the wom the SPCA and Fran The light bulb goe It seems that Fran⬛ isn't so bad after a She actually has a gentle and compassionate si⬛ This convinces M continue on her mission to stop th bullying and, per⬛ the good side of Franka will reveal in the classroom.
Discussion Questions	These questions encourage students to make predictions. They imagine the conversations Mrs. Martin and Franka had regarding Meowy, how Franka came up with the rumor, and why the bullies didn't care if they were proven to be liars.	Students are encouraged to think like bullies. They make predictions and draw conclusions about events that were not actually written in the story.	Students need the discussion questions and a copy of the text to look for the answers. There is an opportunity for open dialogue among students in the form of large group conversations.	Sometimes our life experiences teach us lessons. They allow us to understand things we didn't think we knew. Talking about them brings our beliefs to the surface and reveals our true spirit.	Mrs. Martin and Fr obviously discusse Meowy and her accident with the fishhook. She mus have revealed something that brought Franka to conclusion that M⬛ might have harme⬛ cat. The work of b⬛ can be very destru⬛
Activity 1: **Make A Plan**	Students make a plan to manage the gathering of items for the local animal rescue organization.	Students are on a mission to run an *SPCA Drive* and accomplish all their goals in a matter of four weeks.	Students need a copy of the worksheet, a pencil and time to organize the drive. They join committees, meet, and set out to achieve their goals.	It is one thing to give to those less fortunate but it is much more to organize a drive, gather needed items, and follow it through to completion.	Once students tak⬛ ownership of this without direction management from teacher, wonderfu⬛ changes take plac⬛ Confidence emerg self-esteem blosso and maturity level grow.

AT THE SPCA

Mya and Bobby dropped their bikes in front of the SPCA building. They barged through the door like outlaws running from the police. The clerk at the desk looked up sharply. Her eyes peered over her reading glasses and she said, "Is there something I can help you with?" She had a skeptical look on her face.

Mya quickly inquired about the cat. She started talking very fast and was out of breath. The woman just shook her head and wrinkled her forehead. She tried to make sense of the conversation but looked lost.

Mya continued barking out her words. She said, "Meowy is a gray and orange cat with big green eyes. We want her back. Her owner, Mr. Blanko, brought her here a couple of days ago and he changed his mind. He wants us to bring her home."

The woman blinked at them and looked doubtful after hearing the strange story.

Mya got worried and decided to introduce Bobby. "This is Bobby Blanko, the owner's son. Isn't that right, Bobby?"

Behind her back, she crossed her fingers because she was telling a lie. Mr. Blanko did not want the cat nor did he even know his son and Mya were here. She had heard what happened to animals that stay too long at the SPCA and was praying that Meowy was still there. Bobby just stood next to her with his eyes on his shoes.

The desk clerk, whose name card read April Seeley, began searching through her journal to find the information about Meowy. She was trying to calm the situation down as she slowly licked her finger and rubbed the corner of each page in the book. Her dark hair kept slipping down into her face so she wrapped it up around the back of her left ear. It never stayed. She was snapping her chewing gum like a baseball player. The page seemed to move in slow motion as Mya and Bobby watched and waited.

"It will just be a minute," April said. She scanned the page carefully with her eyes.

"Could you hurry?" Mya urged. "We have to get right home. Bobby's father is waiting for us." She lied again but she was desperate.

Soon another woman came into the room. April explained the story to her. She seemed to be the manager of the SPCA because her nametag had a big star on it. She gazed at the pair with a questioning look on her face. Her hair was pinned back and Mya could easily read the name on her special nametag.

When she saw the last name, it was like a light bulb lit up Mya's brain. Her eyes widened and she exhaled a deep breath of realization, "Hhhhhh."

The woman and April Seeley whispered together. Mya had to think fast. The nametag read Francis Martin, and the only other Martin Mya knew in town was the very obnoxious and mean, Franka Martin. She decided this woman must be Franka's mother.

Something in Mya's mind clicked. She could almost feel her brain develop a new wrinkle as she came up with a conclusion about the rumor. Franka had started the Meowy lies by twisting information she had gotten from this woman who happened to work at the SPCA. It was all beginning to fit together. There were so many coincidences in this story. Mya had to find out if there was a connection.

She asked Mrs. Martin, "Excuse me, but do you have a daughter in Mrs. Braxton's class? I know a Franka Martin. I see your last name and it makes me curious." Then she lied again, "Franka is a very nice girl."

Mrs. Martin's eyes lit up. "Why yes, she is my daughter. And I agree, she is a very nice girl. She is always thinking of others before herself. Sometimes she even volunteers here at the shelter, petting and brushing the animals. She really loves them."

Mya wondered if Mrs. Martin really knew what her daughter Franka was like, but she decided to keep her lips sealed. Now was not the time to make the lady mad at her.

The women talked back-and-forth behind their hands. Bobby and Mya watched them eagerly. Finally Mya said, "We have written permission from Bobby's father, Mr. Blanko, to pick up Meowy."

She didn't know where that idea came from but she hoped there would be a miracle right then. She had no permission slip, and no idea about how she would ever convince these women that Meowy should go home with them. If there was ever a time when she needed a miracle, this was it. She reached down into the bottom of her coat pocket pretending to dig for the permission slip.

Luckily her fingers managed to find a piece of paper she didn't even know was there. She gingerly pulled it up to the top of her pocket so she could get a good look at it and so that no one else would see. It was actually from Chinkley's Produce Market. Mya remembered when Mrs.

Chinkley had written her phone number on it. That was the snowy day when Bonnita and Franka had ambushed her on her way home. She had an idea. She'd pretend this was the permission slip and as she was handing it to them, she'd "accidentally" drop it between the bookcase and the counter where the women were standing. It would take them a while to find it and by then she and Bobby could dash into the pet hotel, grab Meowy, and run. The women would have to scramble to find the slip but, by then, she and Bobby would have Meowy. In her mind, it wasn't really stealing. Meowy did belong to Bobby, sort of.

"We are kind of in a hurry. Can we take her now?" she asked enthusiastically since she had a workable plan.

April turned the page to where she saw a yellow sticky note attached to the place near Meowy's name. Someone had stuck it to the SPCA ledger. "It looks like there is a slight problem," said April, "but you are lucky. I see that someone put a claim on her this afternoon and hasn't shown up yet to take her. It says here she had a fishhook stuck in her lip and she was brought here because she was too much trouble to take care of. A neighbor caused the fishhook problem. Well, it looks like she is still in Cage 27 and she is doing just fine."

Mya began looking down at *her* shoes now. She never gave Meowy the fishhook problem. Why, she and Momma actually saved the cat from starvation and infection. And more than that, their intervention rescued the cat from the throws of death. They were heroes because

they removed that darn hook.

Mrs. Martin reached out her hand to ask for the paper. "Let me see your permission slip," she said. She wanted proof that Bobby was to take Meowy back. Mya's hands began to sweat. She looked at Bobby. His face was totally white and he looked as if he was going to throw up any minute. He buried his chin deeper in his chest.

Then suddenly, the miracle Mya wished for happened. The door swung open. Mya was standing at the counter lifting the paper out of her pocket, when she and everyone in the room automatically turned their heads to see who had suddenly come in. She couldn't believe her eyes!

"Mya, what are you doing here? And Bobby? You are the last two people I expected to see here," the woman said as she closed the door. She looked very surprised but Mya was even more surprised. Her eyes were the size of quarters. Her wish had come true better than she could ever have imagined.

It was Momma! She grabbed her daughter by the shoulders and looked square in her eyes and said, "I was planning a birthday surprise for you, since today is your eleventh birthday. But I think you've spoiled it."

Mya couldn't believe her ears. She couldn't even talk. All she did was listen to Momma's unbelievable words. She had totally forgotten her own birthday because of all the problems she was trying to deal with. Momma said, "Just the other day, Mr.

Blanko told me that he had brought his cat here because he didn't want to be bothered by an animal that was going to cost him money. He said he didn't like cats anyway, and I knew how much you and I loved her. I decided she would make a great surprise birthday gift."

Big tears started rolling down Mya's cheeks. She fell into Momma's wonderful arms and hugged her like she was never going to see her again. She did, however, remember to tuck the paper back into her pocket. Now everything would be ok.

"Do you mind a gift that is not a surprise anymore, Mya?" asked Momma. "We had such a happy time together when we saved the cat from the fishhook. I could tell you fell in love with her as did I. "

"Oh, Momma, I love you," Mya cried. She was so very happy that Momma had planned such a wonderful surprise. She never even dreamed she could have such good luck. "No, I don't mind at all," she said. "That is why Bobby and I came. We are here to claim Meowy and bring her back home. Wow, I never in a million years thought she would be my cat." Mya wasn't ready to tell Momma the whole truth yet.

"OK then, we'll take Meowy Blanko-McGreggor home with us," Momma said to the caretakers with a smile. "She is the cat I asked you to hold for me."

The women had been attentively listening to this story unfold. Mrs. Martin looked confused. She checked the yellow sticky note and, sure enough, the name McGreggor was on it. She escorted the kids and Momma to the cage.

As they arrived, Mya noticed something very different about Meowy. That cat was meowing her head off. She was howling so wildly that she didn't even notice the two kids staring at her through the bars of her cage.

Suddenly, she heard Mya's voice say her name. She stopped. Her green eyes focused on Bobby and Mya peering at her. That's when she began purring as loud as she could. She obviously missed her family and friends. Then she looked straight at Mya and blinked her eyes. Mya, of course, blinked back.

Mrs. Martin said, "Guess we know why her name is Meowy! It will cost you seventy-five dollars to adopt her."

Momma handed the money to the woman and Mya grabbed Meowy and hugged her close to her heart. Then she shared her with Bobby, who held her gently and talked to her in baby talk like he always did.

As the woman turned to walk away, Mya knew Franka Martin's lies and rumors had just been wiped out by a miracle. *Good* had overcome evil once again. It was just like in the stories she loved to read.

At the SPCA

Discussion Questions

 Mya was a very smart girl. She noticed the nametag on Francis Martin's sweater. She put two and two together and concluded that Franka and Francis were related. She thought that they probably were mother and daughter and proceeded to find out if it was true. What conversations probably went on between mother and daughter Martin when Meowy was brought to the SPCA?

 Think like a bully. Tell how Franka and Bonnita came up with the rumor that said that Mya was a cat killer.

 Why didn't Franka and Bonnita worry that the truth would someday come out? They knew that Mya did not do this terrible deed. Why didn't they just give up on bullying Mya?

SPCA Drive

Mya and Bobby visited the SPCA to rescue Meowy from being adopted by strangers. Most importantly, Mya wanted to use the cat to dispel the awful gossip that had been started by Franka.

The SPCA is a wonderful organization that adopts out animals to people who want them. It is a non-profit organization, which means it is totally dependent on people like Momma who pay to take unwanted animals home. Since the SPCA depends on donations from people to feed and care for its animals, this activity will be a chance for your class to make people aware of how needy these abandoned animals are.

Unfortunately, more and more animals continue to be brought to the Humane Society because people cannot or will not take care of them. Perhaps there are animal sanctuaries in your area that need your help. Look around and select the organization that you would like to sponsor.

In this activity, your class will organize a food drive to collect and then deliver food to the local Humane Society. Since the drive may take a period of weeks, it is the only activity listed in Unit 14. Students may continue to Unit 15 while this project is carried out to completion.

On the next page is a list of committees. Join one, to show that you care about unwanted animals. These organizations need different types of items such as food, toys, cleaning materials, leashes, money, or comfort items. The list is endless. The need is endless. It is time to get started.

Here is your task:
First, have an election. Students, who wish to be in a leading role, can run for the position of Director and Assistant Director of the Drive. Here are their job descriptions.

JOB DESCRIPTIONS FOR COMMITTEE HEADS
Director: Manages committees and their tasks, sets timeline for drive

Assistant Director: Manages deadlines and co-manages committee tasks

Next, join a committee and begin the process of collecting items for the drive. Choose one or more of the committees below, and sign up. Each committee has room for four members. Have fun on this important mission. Be proud of yourself for volunteering because you are now officially a "take-charge" person. Volunteering time and energy to save and care for abandoned animals is no small thing.

Committee Names and Descriptions	Volunteer's Name	Volunteer's Name	Volunteer's Name	Volunteer's Name
PORTERS: view SPCA for ific needs and te information				
TER MAKERS: gn and hang posters nounce drive				
WRITERS: e ads to place on ol website				
OUNCERS: advertisements on stem				
LECTORS: ct and store food				
NTERS: inventory count items				
BETWEENS: n SPCA and school fill requests				
TER WRITERS: ose and deliver ted information rents, school, principal				
ORDERS: d and post mplishments				
GNERS: n charts that report imal adoptions ommittee mplishments				
VOLUNTEERS: te time at SPCA for and playing animals				
-FOOD LECTORS: ge Needed ions other than food				
NSFER TEAM: for and deliver to the SPCA				

Unit 15:

KINDNESS WINS OUT

STORY #15 SUMMARY

Meowy Saves the Day

Mya dispels the gossip by bringing Meowy to class. The cat proves to be very much alive and plays a big part in destroying the bullies' power once and for all. Mya's writing is revealed and the class celebrates her strengths. The bullies are exposed and they begin to value Mya's courage.

Lesson	Objectives	Student Goals	Materials and Lesson	Insights	Author's Message
Story #15 Meowy Saves the Day	Students read that Momma and Mya enjoy a party to end all birthday parties. Meowy goes to school with Mya to undo the damage. Students read how the bullies' "reign of terror" disintegrates right before Mya's eyes.	Students identify with Mya's confidence as Meowy's classroom appearance restores her reputation. They notice that her image is bolstered when Mrs. Braxton praises Mya for extending kindness to the wounded creature. They observe that the bullies' credibility is destroyed.	Students need a copy of the text. It can be read aloud to them, or they can read it silently. Small groups can also read together.	In the end good overcomes evil, as it is in the natural way of things.	All the loose ends are tied up as the story ends. We sense that the bullies eventually pay for their poor judgment. They begin to show signs of respect for Mya. Perhaps they had it all along.
Discussion Questions	These questions encourage students relate to Momma's new-found appreciation for her daughter, identify with Meowy's life as it paralleled Mya's, and think about lessons learned from Mya and her dealings with girl bullies.	Readers are taught lesson after lesson about respect and acceptance. They analyze what changes took place and why.	Students need the discussion questions and a copy of the text to look for the answers. There is an opportunity for open dialogue among students in the form of large group conversations.	The more we appreciate and accept ourselves as deserving and contributing human beings, the more others will follow our lead.	All things will turn out well if we look at our problems as opportunities from which to grow to improve our lives.
Activity 1: Creating a Kindness Place	Students create banners to hang around the room as messages of kindness learned from the story. These statements reinforce new beliefs and display, in a bold way, that a change in self-respect has taken place in this classroom.	Students make these banners to announce to the school that this classroom has changed its beliefs. These new attitudes include self-acceptance, self-respect, and the adoption of compassion toward one another.	Students need the worksheet and a dictionary. They also need art materials such as paper, markers, paint, and glue. They design banners, write bold statements, and hang them in the room to show others their new respectful attitudes.	Affirmations can change beliefs. Reading and rereading them will create this change. Forgiveness underlies acceptance of others. In this classroom, there is an overwhelming intolerance for bullies.	These colorful and attractive messages of positive regard show a collective change in the climate of the classroom. This change will last throughout the year and perhaps the rest of their lives.

MEOWY SAVES THE DAY

Mya, Momma, and Meowy rushed around the apartment bumping into each other. It was the next morning and time to get ready for school and work. Momma planned to go in a little later so she could drive Mya and Meowy to school. They were all very tired that morning. They had stayed up late the night before enjoying each other's company, and celebrating Mya's eleventh birthday.

Momma had invited Mr. Blanko, Bobby, and Mrs. Chinkley to the party. Momma made a great meal of spaghetti and meatballs, salad, and some wonderful Italian bread. Mrs. Chinkley supplied the birthday cake. It was Mya's favorite, carrot cake, made with fresh grated carrots from Chinkley's market. And, of course, Mrs. Chinkley made hot chocolate to go with the cake. Bobby brought Meowy's old toys all wrapped up as if they were new. Meowy fell in love with them all over again and played under the table during dinner.

Everyone sang "Happy Birthday" to Mya and she blew out her candles. Mr. Blanko was actually glad Meowy was back. He was tired of watching Bobby moping around the house looking sad and lonely. He presented Mya with a paper collage of Meowy. His artist-sister, Felicia Blanko, had done the portrait of the cat by cutting and pasting layers of paper together. Mya unwrapped it with squeals of joy and hung it above the kitchen table. It was just beautiful. Most of the other gifts were for the cat. But the best present of all was Meowy, herself. That was one gift Mya didn't have to open and she could play with it over and over.

After the party, Momma and Mya enjoyed being with the cat until very late that night. They also talked and talked, for the first time in a long time. It was a conversation Mya had only dreamed about in the past.

For her, Momma had always seemed untouchable. She was always distant, as if her mind was somewhere else, and not on

Mya. But now things were different. Meowy had brought them together and it seemed she had placed a magical spell on them. They were both attracted to each other and to this lovely cat.

Mya was thrilled that she could finally tell Momma about everything that had happened to her since they moved to town. She poured her heart out explaining about Franka and Bonnita. She told Momma all the unhappy details she had kept to herself for far too long. They discussed the sad phone call Momma had gotten from Jack, Mya's dad, just before they moved. Mya told Momma about how she listened outside the bedroom door, guarding her like a watchdog that night. Momma just hugged Mya with tears trickling down her face.

She told Momma about the bridge incident, the ambush on the way to Chinkley's, and the attack on Steven. The worst was the tearful story she sobbed through as she repeated the rumor about being called a cat killer. She revealed her plan to get Meowy from the SPCA and that she had almost lied. That's when Momma wrapped Mya in her arms so tightly that she felt loved for the first time in her life. That's when she knew everything would be all right.

Momma admitted that she had thought about adopting a cat for Mya before she bumped into Mr. Blanko. Then when he told her he had taken Meowy to the SPCA, she decided to adopt Meowy for her daughter. She had seen the love for this cat in Mya's eyes the night they helped Meowy. She also revealed that she had gotten a call

from Mrs. Chinkley on Mya's birthday. Mya's friend had made the suggestion to get the cat as a gift. That convinced Momma to make the move toward adopting this lovely creature that had brought mother and daughter together.

She called the SPCA and put a hold on Meowy so no one else could adopt her. She wanted the apartment to be pet ready before the cat came home. Momma had spent her day off secretly shopping for cat furniture and setting a bed and litter box in a corner of the kitchen. She cooked all day, too. She wanted it to be a wonderful surprise for her caring and kindhearted daughter.

It had been a lovely evening for all three of them. They all slept very soundly. Meowy snoozed happily between Mya and Momma that night, in Momma's cozy old overstuffed bed. It was like heaven for Mya. She couldn't ever remember sleeping that soundly in Momma's comforting arms.

Before they left for school, Momma made an important call to Mrs. Braxton to ask permission for Meowy to make a visit. Mrs. Braxton wasn't too shocked when Momma explained the circumstances for Meowy's visit. It seemed that the teacher had overheard a few students talking about Mya but she never gave it another thought. She was, however, very upset over Franka's and Bonnita's role in passing rumors and it distressed her that they had caused Mya so much sadness.

Momma received permission and they left for school. With Meowy in a cat carrier,

Mya gave Momma a great big hug. Off they went to school and, when they arrived, Mya gave Momma a warm kiss and climbed out of the car. She thanked her for everything and carried Meowy in.

As she looked up the stairway to her classroom, she saw Steven waiting for her at the top. The hallway was empty and lessons were underway. He'd just come out into the hall to get a drink at the water fountain. He was happily surprised to see her climbing the stairs.

"Is that the cat you supposedly killed?" Steven asked with a smile on his face. He grabbed for the cage, to help her as she reached the top stair. "She looks alive to me," he said with a great laugh. "I can't wait to see the look on all their faces when you walk in the room with this cat. I hope they notice your best and only classroom friend beside you, helping to prove your innocence. Let's go in and show them."

Mya was very happy to have Steven stand with her as she entered the room. All eyes turned toward them as they opened the door. Meowy seemed to know how important she was that day. As they walked in, she straightened up and wrapped her tail around her front feet. She quietly stared back at the class. She seemed to be looking for two sets of eyes near the back of the room that glared at her with shock, anger, and rage.

Mrs. Braxton broke the silence. She was standing at the front of the class near the overhead projector. It looked as though she had just started a lesson and was ready to

share something with the class. There was writing projected up on the screen. Mya looked up at the writing. Something was very familiar about it. Then Mya realized it was *her* handwriting. Mrs. Braxton had made a copy of her report about bullies and was showing it to the class! She looked at Mrs. Braxton, stretched her eyes wide open, and under her breath said, "Oh my gosh."

Mrs. Braxton looked at Mya, then at Franka and Bonnita, and finally at the cat. She focused in on Mya and gave her an assuring wink. She walked over and gently put her arm around Mya's shoulders and said, "Well, Mya, what have we here? Is this your new cat? I heard this wonderful story about you and your special act of kindness toward this lovely creature. I was told that you rescued this beautiful orphaned cat from starvation when you helped remove a fishhook from her lip. What a wonderful act of kindness."

Then Mrs. Braxton's eyes darted toward Bonnita and Franka who, by now, had slunk down in their chairs. They were covering their eyes with their hands. It looked like they were trying to be invisible, as if they thought that not seeing the class meant the class couldn't see them.

Once they heard what Mrs. Braxton said about Meowy, every eye in the room had shifted toward the bullies. At this point, Meowy let out a really loud "ME-OW." She startled everyone, including the bullies who put down their hands to look at the cat. As they looked up, they noticed the disgusted stares of the class. Every face seemed to say, "Now we know how mean you two really are. What liars! You tried to make Mya look like a cat killer when, all along, she actually showed kindness toward a helpless animal. She saved its life. How could you?"

Franka and Bonnita just cringed. Meowy gloated. Mya looked over at Steven and he grinned back at her and through his smiling teeth he whispered, "It is about time. Looks like the bullies finally have been stopped!"

Mrs. Braxton walked back over to the overhead projector and quietly wrote herself a reminder on a sticky sheet. She jotted down a message to herself to remember to call Mrs. Martin and Mrs. Campbell. It was time for a parent meeting about bullying. She set her gaze on Franka and then Bonnita as she wrote, hardly looking at the paper. They got the message. They knew she was writing something about them. They knew they were in big trouble. They both swallowed hard and just looked down at their desks.

Then Mrs. Braxton asked Mya, Steven, and Meowy to have a seat. Meowy stared back at the girls from the pillow that had been set out for her on the counter. She kept her eyes on Franka and Bonnita for a long time. It was as if she knew that they had made Mya's fifth grade life miserable.

The teacher began, "Boys and girls, before Mya came in, we were working on our writing lesson. I was about to show you a sample of an opinion paper. Luckily, I found a terrific example right on my desk. I would like to use it as a model, to teach you all how to write your own opinion papers. Remember the bully book you read last week? Well, you are going to write your opinions about bullies, based on that book. You will focus on how much damage bullies can do to innocent people by the hurtful things they say." She looked up at the class. Everyone was riveted to her words. Then she snatched a look back at Franka and Bonnita and went on.

She pointed at the screen and said, "The author of this writing is someone here in our room. It is a person who obviously knows the damage bullies can do and cleverly writes down her feelings. In fact, she persuades the reader how wrong bullying is. Now let's read this paper."

Mrs. Braxton continued as Mya's mind whirled around the teacher's words. She could hardly hold down her excitement about the way things were unfolding. It felt just like she had just taken a big gulp of bubbly soda and the fizzy liquid was tickling her nose and mouth. She barely could contain her joy and pride about what she had written. A few of the kids must have guessed that she was the author because they turned around and looked her way as Mrs. Braxton went on talking.

When her mind grabbed onto Mrs. Braxton's words again, she heard, "...and the author is none other than our very own, Mya."

A cheer started at Steven's desk. She looked over at him and saw the biggest smile. She watched his hands strike each other over and over again. Then, slowly, the other kids joined in the clapping. First Zoey clapped, then Billy, and finally the others. She even heard clapping behind her. To her unbelieving eyes, there were two clappers she never expected to join in. Not in her wildest dreams did she think Bonnita and Franka would clap for her! Even Mrs. Braxton seemed surprised.

Mya shook her head in disbelief and suddenly caught sight of Meowy in the corner of her eye. She turned full face toward the cat and there, as if on command, was the familiar green eyed-blink. Mya just smiled a big contented smile and blinked back at the beautiful cat.

Discussion Questions

 Momma changed her attitude toward Mya. She not only acquired Meowy as a gift for Mya, but they became closer as they shared and cried over the events of Mya's bullied life. What changes did Momma see in Mya?

 Meowy seemed to understand how Mya felt as she was bullied and tortured by Bonnita and Franka. How did this happen?

 Bullies are everywhere. They can be adults. They can be family. They can be animals. They can be boys and, as we know, they can definitely be girls. What is the most important thing Mya taught you about dealing with girl bullies? What did doing these activities teach you about yourself?

Creating a Kindness Palace

With the help of a very special cat, Mya turned her life around. She had many things to be thankful for and she learned several lessons about the power of kindness. Kindness changes people's lives for the better.

This last activity involves turning your classroom into a *Kindness Palace*. You will fill it with banners hanging from the ceiling, the lights, and covering the walls. Each banner will send a message to all who enter. The message is: *Kindness Rules Here!*

Here is your task:

Use pencils, markers, crayons, paint, and 12x18 construction paper to create banners. Design your banner. Illustrate it with pictures (draw or use magazines) and words to show your message of kindness. Reading Mya's stories and doing the many activities after each one, have given you plenty of ideas for the message on your banner.

Here are some suggestions:

■ Always treat others with respect.

■ Bullies don't pick on strong people.

■ Like yourself and be proud.

■ Use a pencil to sketch out your design. Make sure all words are spelled correctly and that your writing is totally readable.

■ Have it checked by the teacher and then color or paint it. Use bold, strong colors to express your message. Outline the letters in black marker so people can easily read it.

■ Hang the banners all over the room, like the banners that decorate palaces.

■ Cover your door with a large sheet of butcher paper. On it, design a mural that sums up how the class feels about bullying as a result of reading Mya's story. Make a pledge to end bullying forever. Write a statement that implies that we must treat everyone with the respect they deserve. You can put the word *BULLIES* in the center of a circle with a diagonal line through it. Or you can make a sign that says, *Bullies Not Allowed Here!* Let the message be clear.

Take a lesson from Mya. When she made her plan to stop Franka and Bonnita, she decided that bullies' lies are very hurtful and they destroy lives. Her mission was to stop the tormenting once and for all. And she did!

Author's Note

The bullies in this fictional story are very much like real-life bullies. They team up and cause pain and sadness wherever they go. Their goal is to hurt people and make their victims feel helpless against them. Mya, luckily, was a strong person who refused to take the role of the victim. She refused to cringe in the shadow of their tormenting behaviors from the start. She thwarted them from the incident on the bridge to the cat killer rumor.

Her friends, Mrs. Chinkley and Steven, built up her confidence and encouraged her to stand up for herself. They gave her the courage to take back her power. She did not wish to be at the mercy of bullies ever again. She knew she deserved to be treated with dignity. Momma sensed this, too. She realized that Mya deserved her respect and understanding as well. Momma saw her daughter change before her eyes. She watched a withdrawn child grow up and demonstrate a take-charge attitude. She realized her own sad life had overshadowed her daughter's loneliness. Momma decided to make things right.

In the real world, bullies eventually are stopped. If they continue bullying into adulthood, like Mr. Calhoon, they find themselves friendless and lonely. Their lives are miserable and sad because all they really have is the growing feeling of dislike for themselves. They are misguided into thinking that people respect them for their strength when, in truth, people are afraid of them and pity them. Bullies eventually realize that they are the weakest of all. They are left with the lies they have told themselves about being the strongest. In the end, bullies lose out. Unless there is an intervention that stops them (like Mya's), bullies continue to be bullied by their own lack of self-love.

And self-love is what actually brought Mya to end her own torment. She knew that she did not deserve to be bullied but was worthy of being treated with respect and dignity, just like everyone else. Good overcame evil once again.

REFERENCES

Andrews, L. V. (1997). *Love and Power*. New York: Harper Collins Publishers, Inc.

Brach, T. (2003). *Radical Acceptance: Embracing Your Life With the Heart of a Buddha.*
New York: Bantam Dell.

Bristol, C. M., & Sherman, H. (1992). TNT: *The Power Within You*. New York: Fireside.

Fauntas, I. C., & Pinnell, G. S. (2001). *Guiding Readers and Writers: Grades 3-6.*
Portsmouth, NH: Heinemann.

Gawain, S. (2003). *Reflections in the Light: Daily Thoughts and Affirmations*. Novato, CA: Nataraj
Publishing.

Hay, L. (2004). *You Can Heal Your Life*. Carlsbad, CA: Hay House, Inc.

McCroskey, J. C. (1993). *An Introduction to Rhetorical Communication: Sixth Edition*. Englewood
Cliffs, NJ: Prentice-Hall, Inc.

McCroskey, J. C. (1968). *An Introduction to Rhetorical Communication: Teacher's Manual.*
Englewood Cliffs, NJ: Prentice-Hall, Inc.

Peterson, R. (1992). *Life in a Crowded Place: Making a Community*. Portsmouth, NH: Heinemann
Educational Books, Inc.

Prochnow, H. (1942). *Public Speaker's Treasure Chest*. New York: Harper & Brothers Publishers.

Rasinski, T. V. (2003). *The Fluent Reader*. New York. Scholastic Professional Books. -Delete

Sharmat, M.W. (1991). T*he Bully on the Bus: The Kids on the Bus No. 3*. New York:
HarperCollins.

Shearin Karres, E. V. (2004). *Mean Chicks, Cliques, and Dirty Tricks*. Avon, MA: Adams Media.

Tipping, C. C. (2002). *Radical Forgiveness: Making Room for a Miracle*. Marietta, GA:
Global 13 Publications, Inc.

Williamson, M. (2002). *Everyday Grace: Having Hope, Finding Forgiveness, and Making Miracles.*
New York: Riverhead.

Young, S. (1994). *The Scholastic Rhyming Dictionary*. New York: Scholastic, Inc.